CHARTING
THE BIBLE
CHRONOLOGICALLY

ED HINDSON & THOMAS ICE

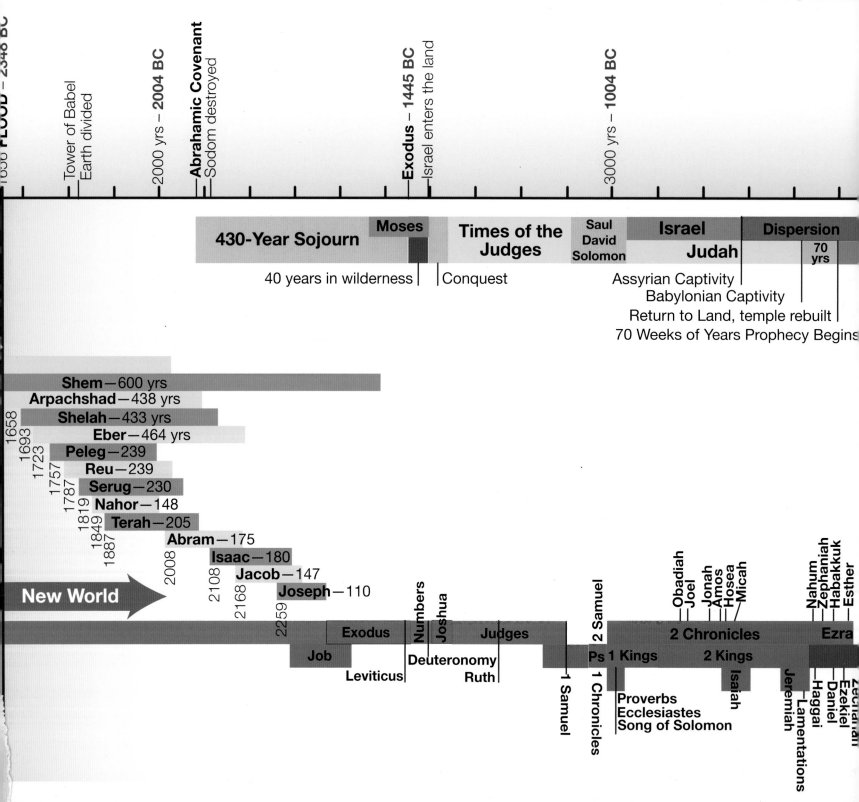

A Timelin

FLOOD – 2348 BC

Tower of Babel
Earth divided

2000 yrs – 2004 BC

Abrahamic Covenant
Sodom destroyed

Exodus – 1445 BC
Israel enters the land

3000 yrs – 1004 BC

430-Year Sojourn | **Moses** | **Times of the Judges** | Saul David Solomon | **Israel** | **Dispersion**
| | | | | **Judah** | 70 yrs

40 years in wilderness | Conquest
Assyrian Captivity
Babylonian Captivity
Return to Land, temple rebuilt
70 Weeks of Years Prophecy Begins

Shem — 600 yrs
Arpachshad — 438 yrs
Shelah — 433 yrs
Eber — 464 yrs
Peleg — 239
Reu — 239
Serug — 230
Nahor — 148
Terah — 205
Abram — 175
Isaac — 180
Jacob — 147
Joseph — 110

1658
1693
1723
1757
1787
1819
1849
1887
2008
2108
2168
2259

New World

Numbers
Joshua

Obadiah
Joel
Jonah
Amos
Hosea
Micah

2 Samuel

Nahum
Zephaniah
Habakkuk
Esther

Exodus | Judges | 2 Samuel | **2 Chronicles** | Ezra

Job
Leviticus
Deuteronomy
Ruth

1 Samuel

Ps 1 Kings
1 Chronicles

2 Kings

Isaiah

Jeremiah

Haggai
Daniel
Ezekiel
Lamentations

Proverbs
Ecclesiastes
Song of Solomon

ETERNITY PAST

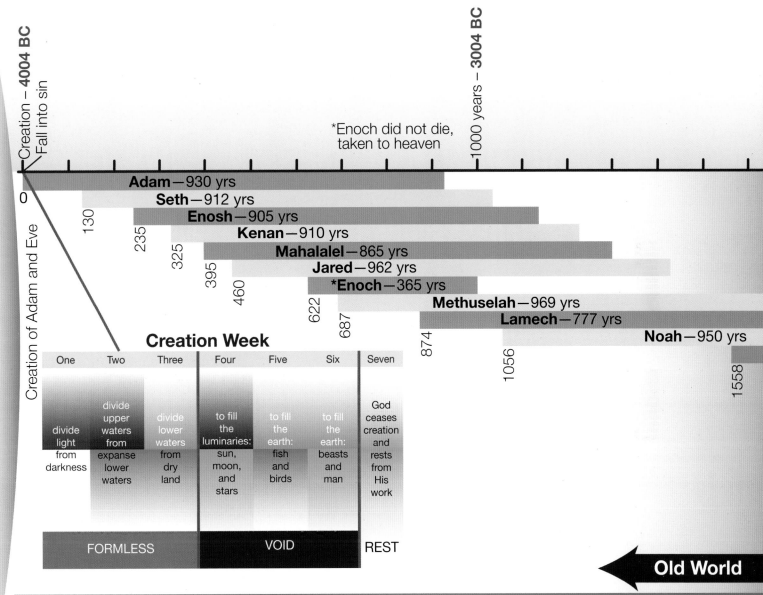

Creation – **4004 BC**
Fall into sin

Creation of Adam and Eve

*Enoch did not die,
taken to heaven

1000 years – **3004 BC**

0

Adam—930 yrs
Seth—912 yrs
Enosh—905 yrs
Kenan—910 yrs
Mahalalel—865 yrs
Jared—962 yrs
***Enoch**—365 yrs
Methuselah—969 yrs
Lamech—777 yrs
Noah—950 yrs

130
235
325
395
460
622
687
874
1056
1558

Creation Week

One	Two	Three	Four	Five	Six	Seven
divide light from darkness	divide upper waters from expanse lower waters	divide lower waters from dry land	to fill the luminaries: sun, moon, and stars	to fill the earth: fish and birds	to fill the earth: beasts and man	God ceases creation and rests from His work

FORMLESS	VOID	REST

Old World

Genesis Covers a Period of 2369 Years

the Bible

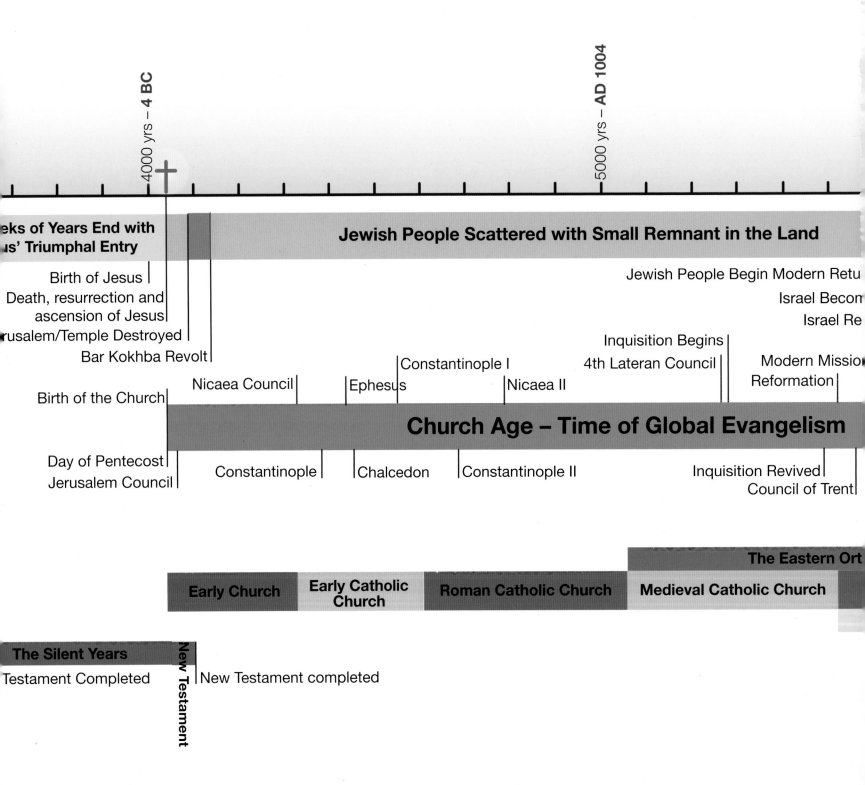

4000 yrs – 4 BC

5000 yrs – AD 1004

eks of Years End with
us' Triumphal Entry

Jewish People Scattered with Small Remnant in the Land

Birth of Jesus

Death, resurrection and
ascension of Jesus

usalem/Temple Destroyed

Bar Kokhba Revolt

Jewish People Begin Modern Retu

Israel Becom

Israel Re

Inquisition Begins
4th Lateran Council

Constantinople I

Modern Missio
Reformation

Nicaea Council

Ephesus

Nicaea II

Birth of the Church

Church Age – Time of Global Evangelism

Day of Pentecost
Jerusalem Council

Constantinople

Chalcedon

Constantinople II

Inquisition Revived
Council of Trent

The Eastern Ort

Early Church | **Early Catholic Church** | **Roman Catholic Church** | **Medieval Catholic Church**

The Silent Years

New Testament

Testament Completed

New Testament completed

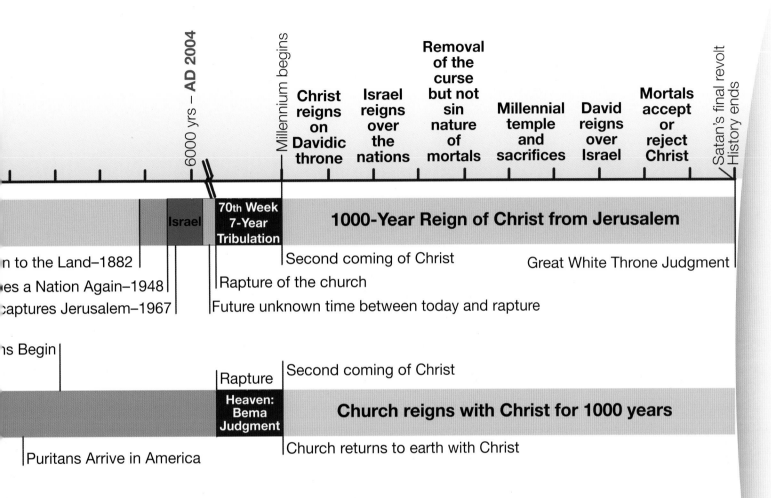

6000 yrs – AD 2004

Millennium begins

Christ reigns on Davidic throne

Israel reigns over the nations

Removal of the curse but not sin nature of mortals

Millennial temple and sacrifices

David reigns over Israel

Mortals accept or reject Christ

Satan's final revolt
History ends

Israel

70th Week 7-Year Tribulation

1000-Year Reign of Christ from Jerusalem

n to the Land–1882

es a Nation Again–1948

captures Jerusalem–1967

Second coming of Christ

Rapture of the church

Future unknown time between today and rapture

Great White Throne Judgment

ns Begin

Second coming of Christ

Rapture

Heaven: Bema Judgment

Church reigns with Christ for 1000 years

Puritans Arrive in America

Church returns to earth with Christ

ETERNITY FUTURE

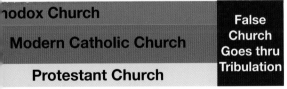

hodox Church

Modern Catholic Church

Protestant Church

False Church Goes thru Tribulation

- Anglicanism
- Lutheranism
- Reformed
- Baptist
- Methodist
- Evangelicalism
- Pentecostalism
- Charismatic

- Liberalism
- Cults

CHARTING THE BIBLE CHRONOLOGICALLY

ED HINDSON & THOMAS ICE

HARVEST HOUSE PUBLISHERS
EUGENE, OREGON

Cover by Dugan Design Group, Bloomington, MN

The illustrations in the charts on pages 16-17, 95, and 140 were originally created by Norma Lane, Legacyroad Solutions, Colorado Springs, Colorado, for use in the Harvest House book Charting the End Times.

CHARTING THE BIBLE CHRONOLOGICALLY
Copyright © 2016 by Ed Hindson and Thomas Ice
Published by Harvest House Publishers
Eugene, Oregon 97402
www.harvesthousepublishers.com

ISBN 978-0-7369-6437-1

Library of Congress Cataloging-in-Publication Data
Names: Hindson, Edward E., author.
Title: Charting the Bible chronologically / Ed Hindson and Thomas Ice.
Description: Eugene, Oregon : Harvest House Publishers, 2016.
Identifiers: LCCN 2016010553 (print) | LCCN 2016030785 (ebook) | ISBN
    9780736964371 (hardcover) | ISBN 9780736964388 ()
Subjects: LCSH: Bible—History of Biblical events.
Classification: LCC BS635.3 .H56 2016 (print) | LCC BS635.3 (ebook) | DDC
    220.95002/02—dc23
LC record available at https://lccn.loc.gov/2016010553

Printed in China

18 19 20 21 22 23 24 / CM-CD / 10 9 8 7 6 5 4

To

DR. JOHN C. WHITCOMB

Defender of the Faith
Biblical scholar, chronologist, theologian, and apologist
whose books and charts have blessed, informed, and challenged us both
for a lifetime of ministry.

Acknowledgments

We want to express our gratitude to Harvest House Publishers for their great support of this project—to Bob Hawkins Jr. for accepting our idea for this project, and especially to Steve Miller, who is the best editor one could hope for.

We are grateful to Dr. Floyd Nolen Jones and his tremendous work on Bible chronology in his book *The Chronology of the Old Testament*. We are also grateful for Dr. John Whitcomb's Old Testament Chronology chart series we found helpful.

We are most grateful to our Lord and Savior, Jesus Christ, for His great gift of salvation and revealing the Father's plan for history in His inerrant Word, the Bible. To God be the glory!

CONTENTS

Introduction

THE IMPORTANCE OF BIBLICAL CHRONOLOGY

THE BIBLE IS UNIQUE when compared with all other "holy books" of the world's religions. One reason the Bible is different is the fact it is the only religious work rooted in past history that also predicts future history. All other religions of the world, unless they rely on the Bible at some point, do not rise or fall on whether they are historically true. These other religions are based upon a philosophy or an ethical way of life and do not stand or collapse on whether they are historically accurate. While the Bible certainly contains theology and ethics, still, it stands on whether what it says actually happened in history or will occur in the future. Because the Bible is God's revelation of Himself and it presents His outline and interpretation of history, it follows that biblical chronology is included in God's Word and is an extremely important element in His revelation to mankind.

Many religions and worldviews believe history is an endless cycle of events continually repeating themselves, and thus they conclude that life is meaningless because, from their perspective, it is going nowhere. By contrast, the biblical view of history is *linear* and not circular. That is, history has a beginning and an ending. It is going somewhere and has purpose and meaning. It began in a garden and is moving toward a city, with a cross in between.

The writer of Hebrews said, "By faith we understand that the worlds were prepared by the word of God, so that what is seen was not made out of things which are visible" (Hebrews 11:3). In this context, the Greek word translated "worlds" (*aiönas*) means "ages" (*aeons*) or "periods." Also, the word "prepared" is better understood as "created." Thus, God is the creator or author of the ages or epochs of history. This could only be if He were the planner and implementer of history. God planned all the events in history and revealed their meaning, purpose, and significance through His Word. This is why studying the chronological data presented in the Bible is so important! As we look carefully at biblical chronology, we gain a proper understanding of the flow of events and their relationship to one another in God's plan.

The Bible tells us who we are as human beings, our purpose for being here on planet Earth, how long we have been here, what we are called to do, and where we are headed in the future. In the chronological revelation within the Bible, we see that God created the heavens and the earth in 6 days a little over 6000 years ago. This indicates that the earth is young in relation to other viewpoints concerning the matter of origins. This is true regardless of all of the false speculations to the contrary by fallen mankind. God has communicated this information to us through His written revelation known as the Bible.

The master foldout chart at the beginning of this book attempts to depict the chronological relationships and progression of important people, places, events, and developments throughout history. We see the life spans of pre-Flood men averaging 930 years, but no one makes it to 1000 years. We see the call of Abraham, the slavery of the Hebrews in Egypt, and the exodus led by Moses. We see the Jewish people's entrance into the land of Israel, Israel's kings, the temples, and the dispersions into the Gentile nations. Christ is born, ministers, dies for the sins of the world, is resurrected, and ascends to heaven. The church is born on Pentecost and the church age is now approaching 2000 years of gospel preaching throughout the world. The uniqueness of the Bible appears again as the book of Revelation discloses the future: The rapture of the church, the 7-year tribulation, Christ's second coming, then Christ's millennial kingdom, followed by the

transition into the eternal state after the Great White Throne Judgment. The final pages of the biblical revelation take us to the new heavens, the new earth, and the new Jerusalem—the glorious holy city of God.

The authors of this book take God's Word seriously, believing that it contains accurate history and a clear revelation of the future. In this book we offer an attempt to chart out those aspects of Scripture that provide us a summary of times and events in God's plan for mankind. Wherever we have a difference of opinion on some minor details, we have deferred to Dr. Ice's chronology on the charts. Our desire is to aid believers in their attempt to grasp the reality of God's Word so that it will help them to trust Him more in the course of living out their daily lives.

The Bible clearly reveals that history is not just a cyclical series of meaningless events. Rather, it teaches us that history is progressing—in a linear manner—through God-ordained happenings that are moving this world toward the goal of the glorification of God for all eternity. The apostle Paul tells us, "For from Him and through Him and to Him are all things. To Him be the glory forever. Amen" (Roman 11:36).

WHY A CHART BOOK ON BIBLE CHRONOLOGY?

THERE'S A POPULAR PROVERB that suggests "a picture is worth a thousand words." If that is true, good charts are worth a thousand words when it comes to illustrating chronological relationships as revealed in the Bible. The value of chronology charts is that they enable us to pinpoint the timing of the events described in Scripture and show their relationship to each other. With a chart, we can summarize a subject or theme that, in written form, might take pages to explain. In this book, you will find virtually all the key chronological information from the Bible and how it relates to the passage of time.

One key distinctive of biblical Christianity is that God knows and reveals the past, the present, and the future (Isaiah 46:8-11). Only God can do that. Thus, the past and future are settled, and are not open to change. This means we can look at the charts in this book with an assurance that the biblical teachings they portray have taken place or will take place precisely as the Bible says. Because God conceived His plan for history before creation, we can have confidence that events from the past and future have and will take place exactly as He has

decreed. Such a realization enables us to fully participate in God's ongoing plan for history with great confidence.

Our prayer is that *Charting the Bible Chronologically* will enable you to gain a better grasp of what Scripture reveals about what has happened, what is happening, and what will happen in the future.

A Timeline of History According to the Bible

It is often said that the big questions in life are these: Who are you? Where did you come from? And, Where are you going? The Bible has the answers to all three questions. The Lord says,

> Remember this, and be assured; recall it to mind, you transgressors. Remember the former things long past, for I am God, and there is no other; I am God, and there is no one like Me, declaring the end from the beginning, and from ancient times things which have not been done, saying, "My purpose will be established, and I will

accomplish all My good pleasure"; calling a bird of prey from the east, the man of My purpose from a far country. Truly I have spoken; truly I will bring it to pass. I have planned it, surely I will do it (Isaiah 46:8-11).

Because God has revealed Himself through Scripture, an informed believer should clearly know who he is in Christ, where he has come from, and where he is going.

Unless one knows everything, he cannot know anything with certainty because what he thinks he knows may be affected by what he does not know. Because the God of the Bible knows everything, and because He has revealed some things to humanity through His Word, we can have certainty about those things which He has revealed. Biblical Christianity is rooted and grounded upon revelation from God, which is why we can know with certainty what happened at creation and what will happen in the future. God has revealed it in the Scriptures! There are some who say we Christians are bigots because we claim to possess truth and correct knowledge as revealed to us in the Bible. They will never understand why we are so confident that we see specific issues so clearly.

By contrast, the unbeliever's starting point is with the rejection of God's revelation, which is why he cannot understand how anyone can have certainty when it comes to knowledge about the past or the future. Yet the God of the Bible not only claims to have been an eyewitness to creation, He is said to have actually been the One who created the heavens and the earth. Because He is sovereign over the future, He can be certain about what will unfold in the days ahead as well.

The apostle Peter dealt with this very issue in his second and final epistle when he said,

Know this first of all, that in the last days mockers will come with *their* mocking, following after their own lusts, and saying, "Where is the promise of His coming? For *ever* since the fathers fell asleep, all continues just as it was from the beginning of creation." For when they maintain this, it escapes their notice that by the word of God *the* heavens existed long ago and *the* earth was formed out of

water and by water, through which the world at that time was destroyed, being flooded with water. But by His word the present heavens and earth are being reserved for fire, kept for the day of judgment and destruction of ungodly men (2 Peter 3:3-7).

These last-days scoffers, which may even include some from within the church, start by rejecting God's Word. They are said to follow "after their own lusts." The Greek word translated "lusts" is *epithumia* and means "a great desire for something, longing, craving."[1] Unlike our English word *lust*, which always has a negative connotation, this Greek word can denote something that is good. However, in this context, it clearly refers to something evil. It's clear that the scoffers start with their own feelings, thoughts, and inclinations rather than with the Word of God. Therefore, they have corrupt motives that lead to their scoffing about God's knowledge of the past and the future.

In 2 Peter 3:5, the phrase "for when they maintain this," is better translated "for this they deliberately, or willingly, overlook." The text says it is a willful exclusion of past historical events that leads these scoffers to their errant conclusion that "all continues just as it was from the beginning of creation." Their assumption is that Christ will not fulfill His promises regarding the future.

The chronological data in this chart book is based almost exclusively upon what the Bible itself says. We accept this at face value and have built our charts upon a straightforward reading of God's Word. There is a place for critical interaction, but that is left for others. We are simply attempting to lay out what Scripture plainly says about the order in which things have happened, or will take place. For those who trust the Bible as the Word of God, it's vital to know what it says and what the implications are of those statements.

Only in the Bible do we have enough of the proper information in order to compose a chart that provides a comprehensive overview of history. Only God was there when it all began, and He is quite capable of communicating what He did to bring about the heavens and the earth and fill them with His creatures. Only God knows the end from the beginning. Not only that, He has determined our future, and it will surely come to pass. It is those who scoff at the Word of God who offer mere speculation about the past and the future. It is those who believe that present processes are the key to the past and future who hold to uniformitarian speculation. The Bible, on the other hand, provides plenty of information that makes it possible for us to chart the past, present, and future.

The Creation

At some point in eternity past, God created the heavens and the earth in six literal days and rested on the seventh day (Genesis 1:1–2:3; Exodus 20:11), thus establishing the pattern for our seven-day week. Adam was created to rule over and subdue creation, starting with the garden in Eden. Eve was fashioned from Adam's side so that all of Adam's prodigy would have his DNA, resulting in the genealogical solidarity of the human race. It appears that within a short time Adam, influenced by Eve, cast the entire human race into sin by eating the forbidden fruit. Thus, Adam and Eve did not live long in their pre-Fall innocence. Satan and a third of the angels fell into sin before Adam, and probably fell sometime between Genesis 2 and 3.

Before the Flood, the average life span of an individual was 930 years. That doesn't include Enoch, who never died, but instead, was raptured to heaven at the age of 365 years. The amount of knowledge accumulated by people must have been amazing because so many of them lived almost a millennium. The pre-Flood environment was clearly healthier for people than the post-Flood, but the longer life spans also meant that humanity had many more opportunities to descend more and more into sinfulness. As Genesis 6:5 says, "The LORD saw that the wickedness of man was great on the earth, and that every intent of the thoughts of his heart was only evil continually." Further, there was the problem of fallen angels procreating with human women (in the Bible, all angels who are manifest in physical form are male) and producing a hybrid the Bible calls "Nephilim" (Genesis 6:4). The continued procreation of these hybrids would eventually render the human race unsavable because they would corrupt the DNA of Adam. So 1656 years after creation, God brought the global Flood in order to destroy the pre-Flood world and its inhabitants and start over with Noah and his wife, their three sons, and their wives.

The Flood

The Flood was a further cursing of mankind—before it, people lived an average of 930 years, and afterward, the average life span eventually dropped to about 70 to 80 years. Then 166 years later, when Nimrod and others built the Tower of Babel, God caused them to speak different languages so they could not coordinate their efforts to unite in rebellion against Him. The Tower of Babel was an attempt to bring the kingdom of man in opposition to God. About 250 years later, God called Abram out of Ur of the Chaldeans (right in the heart of Babylon) and began to build a counter-response against the kingdom of man. God then made promises to Abraham—through the Abrahamic Covenant—that from him would come a nation, Israel, that would produce the Messiah who would make it possible to offer salvation to mankind.

The Abrahamic Promise

Because the Bible provides numbered genealogies in Genesis 5 and 11, we are able to see how many years it was from creation to the call of Abraham, which was 2083 years, or 1927 BC. While the Abrahamic Covenant was made almost 4000 years ago, the Lord did not create the nation of Israel and put them in their land for another 470 years. The Jews, God's chosen people, have been in the land of Israel since about 1400 BC. After building the Jewish population while they resided in Egypt, God used Moses to lead the nation out in 1446 BC, freeing them from the oppression of one of the most totalitarian governments in the history of the world. After 40 years in the wilderness, Joshua led the people of Israel into the land of Canaan. After that came the times of the Judges, which lasted about 250 years, during which time the nation longed for a king. God gave the people three successive kings that reigned over a unified nation for 120 years.

Then Solomon's son split the nation into two parts—the north and the south. The divided kingdoms went on for another 250 years, until the Northern Kingdom was taken into captivity by the Assyrians in 721 BC on account of persistent idolatry. The Southern Kingdom was taken captive by Babylon about 150 years later, and Jerusalem and Solomon's Temple were destroyed in 586 BC. Seventy years later, about 50,000 of the Jewish people returned from Babylon to the land of Israel and rebuilt the Second Temple.

Most of the Old Testament was written during the time from the exodus until the exile. The last Old Testament book to be written was Malachi, around 430 BC. The period spanning the next 400 years—until the birth of Jesus—is called the silent years or the Intertestamental Period. It is during this time that most of the 69 weeks of years (483 total years) prophesied in Daniel 9:25 transpired.

The New Testament

The birth of Jesus around 4 BC brought new life and hope into Israel. Jesus' public ministry began in AD 29, aided by the ministry of his cousin John the Baptist. Jesus presented Himself to the people of Israel through His teaching ministry, which was accompanied with miracles of all kinds. During His final week on earth before His crucifixion, Jesus fulfilled to the very day the first 69 weeks of years, or 483 years prophesied in Daniel 9:25, when He entered Jerusalem on Palm Sunday (Luke 19:28-44). Four days later, Jesus fulfilled Old Testament prophecy when He was crucified by His own people, placed in a tomb for 3 days and nights, then raised from the dead. After Jesus conquered sin and death, He spent the next 40 days teaching His disciples about the kingdom. Then He ascended into heaven, where He currently makes intercession for the saints. As He ascended, angels declared to the disciples that Jesus will one day return physically to earth (Acts 1:11).

Jesus' death, burial, resurrection, and ascension was not the end of His ministry. In many ways, it was just the beginning. On the Day of Pentecost, Jesus sent the Holy Spirit upon the disciples and others, which led to the founding of the church, the body of Christ (in AD 33). The newly born church grew quickly, spreading first to thousands of Jewish converts within Jerusalem, then to Jews and Gentiles throughout Judea, and then by the end of the book of Acts, to the outer reaches of the known world at that time (Acts 1:8). The first book in the New Testament canon was James, written around AD 45. The final book in the canon of the New Testament—and the entire Bible—was Revelation, written in AD 95 by John while he was on the island of Patmos.

The Fate of Israel

In AD 70, judgment came upon Israel for rejecting Jesus as their Messiah. In August of that year, Roman soldiers destroyed Jerusalem and the Second Temple. The global dispersion of the Jewish people began at this time, although a remnant still lived in the land, which has been the case ever since the beginning of the nation. The Jews within Israel managed to regroup and rise up against the Romans in AD 132 during the Bar Kokhba Revolt. Rome came again and destroyed Jerusalem and sent most of the Jews into the diaspora. The Jews remained largely scattered until a movement began in the 1880s as some began to return and resettle the land. Against all odds, the modern state of Israel was founded in 1948 with less than a million Jews. Today, more than a third of all Jews worldwide have returned to Israel.

Growth of the Church

Meanwhile, the church continued to grow steadily, and around 280 years after her founding, for all practical purposes, she took over the Roman Empire, her greatest adversary. The church became so powerful throughout Europe during the Middle Ages that it dominated civil governments and became very worldly. The Reformation, which generally began in the early 1500s, led to a recovery of the gospel and in many ways a revival of biblical Christianity. The modern Protestant missionary movement began in the late 1700s as all forms of Christianity went on to become the largest religion in the world. Even today the gospel continues to spread rapidly, and it can be said that the gospel message has circled the globe going from west to east and now back to Jerusalem.

Promise of the Future

Today many believers are living in anticipation of the rapture of the church, which will end the current church age and lead to God's end-time program, which includes the national conversion of Israel to Jesus as their Messiah and the saturation of the entire world with the preaching of the gospel during the 7-year tribulation. Jesus will return to planet Earth at the second coming to rescue a converted nation of Israel and will judge unbelievers in preparation for His 1000-year reign from Jerusalem.

During this time, Jesus will reign upon David's throne, while Israel, as His sub-regent, will rule over the nations. The curse that was applied in Genesis 3 and 8 will be totally removed, except death will still be a possibility for some mortals. Worship of the Lord will occur in the Fourth Temple, which, according to Ezekiel, will be brought from heaven. The sacrificial system will also be reestablished for the cleansing of the priests, temple, and implements.

Christ's sacrifice on the cross will continue to be the only basis on which people have their sins forgiven. The church, as the bride of Christ, will rule with Christ during this period (Revelation 3:21). Mortals who are born during the Millennium will still have to trust Christ as their Savior if they want to obtain eternal life.

At the end of the 1000-year reign, Satan will be loosed from the abyss so he can once again deceive the nations. Thousands of unbelieving Gentiles will be attracted to his final rebellion and will surround Jerusalem. The Lord will make short work of these rebels and strike them down with a bolt of lightning from heaven. This will be the last event in all of history.

There will be a transition from history to the eternal state via the Great White Throne Judgment. By the end of history, all believers will have been resurrected and will receive their new, glorified bodies, which will enable us to function for all eternity. All unbelievers from throughout history will then have their day in court. Because they never trusted Christ as their Savior and received forgiveness of their sins, they will be evaluated on the basis of their good works, with God's righteousness being the standard. This means that not one person who rejected Christ will be able to earn their way into heaven. All of them will be cast into the Lake of Fire—for eternity.

At the end of history, the current heavens and earth will be totally destroyed because they are still tainted by sin. God will create new heavens and a new earth completely free of sin. The new earth will have a New Jerusalem where the saints will live forever in unbroken fellowship with God the Father, God the Son, and God the Holy Spirit. Righteousness and evil will be forever separated, and eternity will not be long enough for humanity to thoroughly grasp the glory and greatness of God. For those who have received Jesus as their Savior, the best is yet to come. For unbelievers, there is a terrible future in store for all eternity. This is what the Bible, God's revelation of His plan for history, reveals with absolute certainty.

2

HOW WE GOT OUR BIBLE

THE BIBLE IS THE MOST DETAILED revelation of God and His wonderful plan for the future of mankind. There are other ways He has revealed Himself—through the heavens, through the Lord Jesus Christ, and through the power of the cross to change lives today. But the most detailed revelation He has given is the Bible itself. This amazing book was compiled in the most unusual manner of any book ever written. God the Holy Spirit inspired more than 40 holy men, mostly prophets, to write the 66 books that comprise this library. It contains what we need to know about salvation, how to live the Christian life, the nature and plan of God, the end times, and the second coming of Christ.

No other book has ever been so loved or hated. The Bible has been loved by multitudes through the centuries, many of whom have had life-changing experiences as they read, studied, and followed its timeless principles for living. It has been hated by atheists, freethinkers, and other secularists whose belief systems assume there is no God. If there is no God, then there is no divine inspiration. Never mind that these skeptics cannot explain the remarkable accuracy and consistency of the Bible, which was written over a 1500-year period by mostly ordinary men. The Bible has been the subject of more persecution and book burning than any book in history, yet it is the bestselling book of all time. It is also the only reliable source of information about the future. In fact, the ability of God to write history in advance, which is the definition of prophecy, is one of the proofs of the divine origin of Scripture. Dr. John Walvoord, the dean of prophecy scholars in the twentieth century, identified 1000 prophecies in Scripture, 500 of which have been fulfilled literally. The obvious conclusion is that the 500 yet to be fulfilled, which deal with future end-time events, will also be fulfilled literally.

Because the Bible is the source of all the historical data and prophecies described in this chart book, it's important to understand how the Bible came to be, how it was preserved through the centuries, and how we can be confident that it is the same revelation God gave to man thousands of years ago when it was first written.

An Overview of the Bible

The Bible has two major sections: the Old Testament and the New Testament. Let's look first at the Old Testament.

The Old Testament

There are five basic categories of books in the Old Testament:

1. Law . . . . 5 books—Genesis to Deuteronomy

2. History . . . . 12 books—Joshua to Esther

3. Poetry . . . . 5 books—Job to Song of Solomon

4. Major Prophets . . . . . 5 books—Isaiah to Daniel

5. Minor Prophets . . . . 12 books—Hosea to Malachi

The account of God, creation, man, his origin and fall, the Flood, and the earliest civilizations is presented simply and clearly in the 50 chapters of Genesis, the first book of the Bible. Genesis has been a prime target of critics for years. Their greatest attack has been leveled against the authorship of Genesis—they say, "Moses was too far removed from the original events to speak accurately." These objections dissolve when we understand that "all Scripture is given by inspiration of God" (2 Timothy 3:16 KJV). So it was God who wrote Genesis through Moses.

What's more, archaeological discoveries have indicated that writing is as old as man, which means it is highly probable that Moses had received written accounts of many of the events from those who actually participated in them. The other 38 books of the Old Testament were written during or just after the time they describe. God selected men from various walks of life through whom He "breathed" His Word. Among the writers were priests, prophets, herdsmen, kings, and judges. All worked faithfully, largely without ever having met the others, and yet the whole Bible is one continuous, consistent, and unique message of salvation.

Due to the passage of time and the fragile nature of writing materials such as clay, papyrus, and leather, we do not have the original writings produced by these men. But we do have numerous ancient copies of these writings—copies that are considered extremely reliable. The accuracy of today's Bible text has been significantly confirmed by the Dead Sea scrolls, which, when compared to the current texts, reveal a near-perfect match.

The word *canon*, which means "measuring rod" or "rule," is the title given to those religious writings that have met the exacting standards required for inclusion in the Old Testament. The work of canonizing the Old Testament was done during the days of Nehemiah, Haggai, Zechariah, and Malachi. After Israel's captivity in Babylon, a council of 120 men was formed, with Ezra as its president, for the purpose of reconstructing the worship and religious life of the Jewish people after their return from Babylon. It's possible that this group of spiritual leaders, or certainly their successors, brought together the many religious writings that now comprise the Old Testament. Josephus, a noted Jewish historian, mentions 22 books which this group believed to be divine, and he listed those books. It is significant that the list corresponds exactly with the Old Testament in today's Bibles—our 39 books are exactly the same in content as their 22 books! (Back then, they combined several books, such as 1 and 2 Kings.)

Before a book could be included in the Old Testament, the council asked, "Is it divinely inspired?" "Was it written by a prophet or spokesman for God?" "Is it genuine, and can it be traced back to the time and place as well as the writer?" It's worthwhile to note that Jesus and the apostles quoted from the Old Testament more than 600 times, indicating their approval of the selected texts. It is with utmost confidence, then, that we can accept the Old Testament as God's divinely inspired Word.

Between the Testaments

The first translation of the Hebrew Old Testament into another language was called the *Septuagint*. Seventy scholars were brought to Alexandria, Egypt, to create this Greek translation (hence the name the *Septuagint*, or LXX, or 70). The work began around 280 BC and was completed about 100 years later. This work is significant to us

How We Get Our Bible

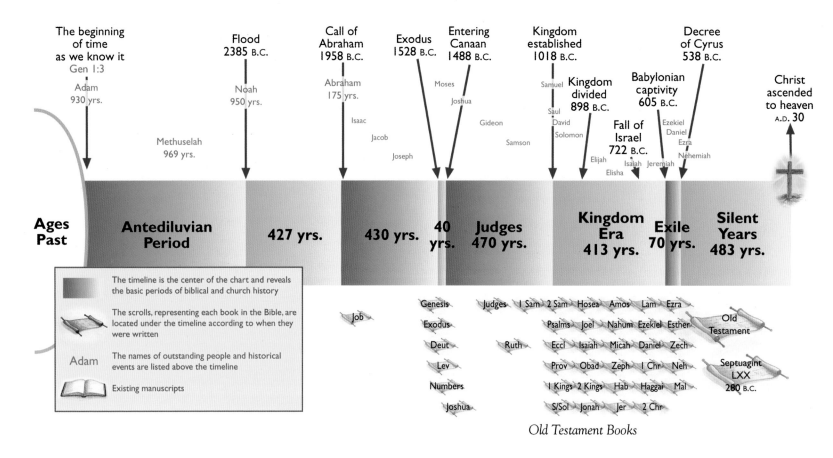

Old Testament Books

because it proves the Old Testament was canonized by this time. It is also important because its agreement with the original Hebrew text shows that the translators took great care to create an accurate work.

When our modern-day Bibles are compared with the ancient Hebrew texts, Greek Septuagint, and Greek texts, very few differences are found. This clearly suggests the Bible has been accurately preserved like no other ancient book.

The *Apocrypha* is the title given to 14 books that are included in the Roman Catholic Bible. These books were written in the era between the Old Testament and the New Testament. They contain fanciful stories and contradictory statements that immediately reveal that they are not

on the same par as Scripture. They have never been accepted by the Jews as inspired writ, were not quoted by Jesus nor any of the apostles, and were not recognized by the early church. They were "slipped in" with a translation of the Greek Septuagint during the fourth century AD and were recognized by the Catholic Church at the Council of Trent in 1546. They have never been accepted by the Protestant church.

The New Testament

The New Testament is not arranged chronologically. The accompanying chart lists the 27 books as they were written, beginning with James about AD 50.

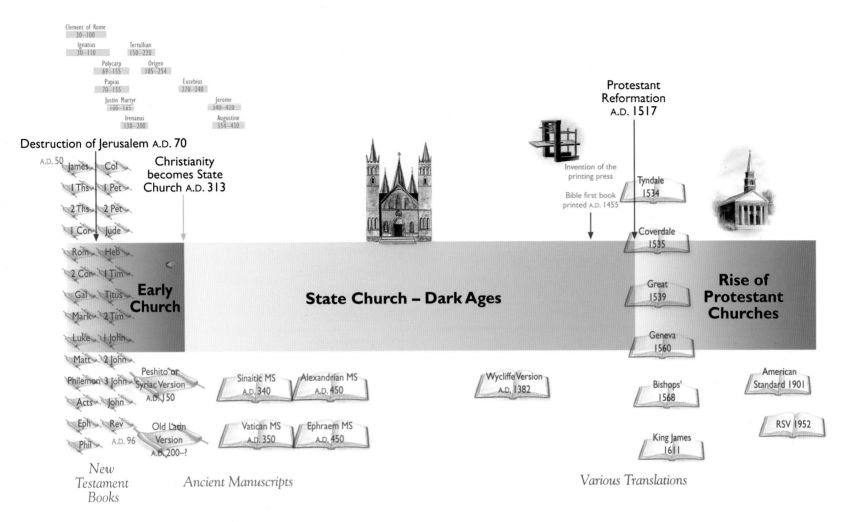

Clement of Rome 30–100
Ignatius 30–110
Tertullian 150–220
Polycarp 69–155
Origen 185–254
Papias 70–155
Eusebius 270–340
Justin Martyr 100–165
Jerome 340–420
Irenaeus 130–200
Augustine 354–430

Destruction of Jerusalem A.D. 70

Christianity becomes State Church A.D. 313

Protestant Reformation A.D. 1517

A.D. 50

James, Col
1 Ths, 1 Pet
2 Ths, 2 Pet
1 Cor, Jude
Rom, Heb
2 Cor, 1 Tim
Gal, Titus
Mark, 2 Tim
Luke, 1 John
Matt, 2 John
Philemon, 3 John
Acts, John
Eph, Rev
Phil

A.D. 96

Early Church

State Church – Dark Ages

Invention of the printing press

Bible first book printed A.D. 1455

Tyndale 1534

Coverdale 1535

Great 1539

Geneva 1560

Rise of Protestant Churches

Peshito or Syriac Version A.D. 150

Old Latin Version A.D. 200–?

Sinaitic MS A.D. 340

Alexandrian MS A.D. 450

Vatican MS A.D. 350

Ephraem MS A.D. 450

Wycliffe Version A.D. 1382

Bishops' 1568

King James 1611

American Standard 1901

RSV 1952

New Testament Books

Ancient Manuscripts

Various Translations

The New Testament is divided into five sections:

1. The Gospels . . . . 4 books—Matthew, Mark, Luke, and John

2. The History of the Early Church . . . . 1 book—Acts

3. Paul's Epistles . . . . 14 books—Romans to Hebrews

4. General Epistles . . . . 7 books—James to Jude

5. Prophecy . . . . 1 book—Revelation

The New Testament's Authority

From the start, the early church used the Old Testament in their services with the same authority as did the Jews in their synagogues. As the New Testament books were completed, they were given the same respect as the prophets or Moses and were used right along with the Old Testament Scriptures. In fact, in 1 Timothy 5:18, the apostle Paul quotes from Luke 10:7, citing it as "scripture." He evidently regarded Luke's Gospel as Scripture before he wrote his great message on biblical inspiration in 2 Timothy 3:16. In 2 Peter 3:1-2, the apostle Peter placed his and the other apostles' writings on par with those of the Old Testament prophets. He also showed in 2 Peter 3:15-16 that he was familiar with Paul's writings and regarded them with the same degree of authority reserved for the Old Testament writers. This seems to be the common perspective of all the early church leaders.

The Original New Testament Manuscripts

The original manuscripts of the New Testament books were written on papyrus, which is the name of an aquatic plant in Egypt. The manuscript material came from this plant, and its fragile nature made it difficult for these manuscripts to survive. During the fourth century, vellum came into use, a much-improved writing material. There are several copies of the New Testament from this era that have survived through today.

Altogether there are more 5000 copies of the New Testament that survive from the ancient world. By comparing these handwritten copies, biblical scholars are able to verify the original text of the Bible with incredible accuracy.

Ancient Translations of the New Testament

The New Testament was originally written in Greek, and the work of translating it into other languages began early.

The Peshito or Syriac translation was written in Syrochaldaic, or Aramaic. Translated before AD 150, it has always been regarded with utmost respect and became the official Scriptures of the Eastern churches. From it, translations have been made into Arabic, Persian, and Armenian.

The Latin Vulgate, translated by Jerome in the fourth century, became the Bible of the Western churches and, for more than 1000 years, was the chief source of nearly every version of the Scriptures made in the West.

There are two important facts confirmed by these ancient translations: One, the New Testament was completed by the second century; and two, the authenticity of our New Testament can be traced back to within 100 years or less of the apostles. Even the book of Revelation, written by John on Patmos in AD 95, was given instant acceptance by the early church as the fitting conclusion to the library of God.

Hundreds of other manuscripts—both versions and translations written into still other languages—appeared during the second and third centuries. These were destroyed by the Roman emperors, particularly Diocletian, who ordered the destruction of the sacred writings of the Christians.

When Emperor Constantine professed Christianity in AD 312, he authorized Eusebius, known as the father of church history, to prepare 50 copies of the Scriptures to be used in churches. The question naturally arose: Which religious books are regarded to be Scripture? Through his research the answer became obvious: the 27 books of the New Testament, because they had been universally accepted since the earliest days of the church. Constantine also found that the books about which there had been some questions did not seem to be such that they should be omitted, for usage had long established their being recognized as inspired Scripture along with the other books. The tests of canonicity were much the same as they were for the Old Testament: Was this written by an apostle or a close associate of an apostle? Does it agree with the doctrine of the Lord and His apostles? Is it genuine with regard to facts, the date of writing, and the author? And, was it accepted for use in the early church? The 27 New Testament books we use today were formally ratified by the Council of Carthage in AD 397, which recognized only the books that had already been used by the church for more than three centuries.

The Ancient Manuscripts of the Bible

The most ancient existing manuscripts of the entire Bible are shown on the "How We Got Our Bible" chart. They comprise only a fraction of those in existence. It has been stated by scholars that we have more than 5800 Greek manuscripts of the New Testament, and 19,000 copies of ancient versions (mostly of the Latin Vulgate). Add those up, and we have around 25,000 manuscripts of all or parts of the

New Testament, not to mention the 1700 fragments of the Hebrew Old Testament and the 350 copies of the Greek Septuagint.

Josh McDowell, in his book *God-Breathed: The Undeniable Power and Reliability of Scripture*, states,

> Once archaeologists completed their search of the Qumran caves—eleven caves in all—almost 1,050 scrolls had been found in about 25,000 to 50,000 pieces (a number that varies depending on how the fragments are counted). Of these manuscripts, about three hundred were texts from the Bible, and many of the rest had direct relevance to early Judaism and emerging Christianity. Every book of the Old Testament was represented, except for the book of Esther, and the earliest copies dated from about 250 BC.[1]

No other ancient document comes even close to having such numbers back up its authenticity.

Sinaitic Manuscript–AD 340

This manuscript, written in Greek, is now in the British Museum. In 1844, Dr. Constantin Tischendorf discovered this manuscript by accident in the Monastery of St. Catherine at Mount Sinai. He saw some pages of it in the hall waiting to be used to light the monastery fires and recognized they might have significance, so he rescued them. Eventually the manuscript was given to the Czar of Russia and, after the Revolution of 1917, it was sold to the British Museum for the sum of $500,000.

Vatican Manuscript–AD 350

This manuscript, written in Greek, is in the Vatican Library in Rome, Italy. It was revealed for the first time in a Vatican Library catalog in 1481. It was not opened to the public until the nineteenth century, after Tregelles, a famous English Bible scholar, was permitted to study it for several days. He claimed that he had memorized it and could reproduce it. Then the pope, in 1889, permitted this manuscript to be photographed and released to the libraries of the world.

Alexandrian Manuscript–AD 450

This was written in Greek, probably in Alexandria, Egypt. It is currently in the British Museum. It was presented to King James I of England in 1627.

Ephraem Manuscript–AD 450

Written in Greek and located in the National Library of Paris, France, this manuscript is thought to have been written in Alexandria. It was scrubbed clear by someone who did not recognize its worth, and the discourses of Ephraem, a Syrian father of the fourth century, were copied on it. It was given to the French Library in Paris, where a student noticed the faint writings underneath the Syrian text. Later, chemicals were applied that helped bring out much of the original writing.

From this point onward in time, we have many other Bible manuscripts, including the Beza Manuscript of AD 550, which is in the Cambridge University Library, Cambridge, England. The Claromontanus Manuscript (AD 550) is in the National Library of Paris. The Washington Manuscript (AD 550) is now in the National Library, Washington, DC.

The writings of the early church fathers comprise a great bridge between the ancient manuscripts and the original New Testament writings. These men were the earliest leaders of the Christian church after the days of the apostles. Some of the most important are listed on the chart along with the time they lived. For the most part they were well-educated men and voluminous writers. They quote repeatedly from the New Testament—for example, Clement referred to Matthew, Luke, Romans, Corinthians, Hebrews, 1 Timothy, and 1 Peter. Ignatius referred to the Gospels as "the word of Jesus." Polycarp, a disciple of the apostle John, in a very short letter that takes only ten minutes to read, quoted from two-thirds of the books in the New Testament. Irenaeus quoted from the New Testament 1800 times, and Tertullian did the same 7200 times. In fact, even though only a small percentage of the writings of the early church fathers have survived to the present day, they still contain all but 11 verses of the New Testament.

This indicates that we can trace the actual words of the New Testament to within a very few years of the original manuscripts.

Various Translations of the Bible

Latin Vulgate–AD 450

Translated by Jerome from Hebrew, Greek, and Latin manuscripts. The Vulgate became the official Bible of the Roman Catholic Church for more than 1000 years.

Wycliffe's Version–1382

John Wycliffe was the first person to translate the Bible into English. He is called "The Morning Star of the Reformation."

Tyndale's New Testament

Translated on the European continent from Erasmus's Greek New Testament (1519 and 1522 editions).

Coverdale Bible–1535

Translated by Miles Coverdale, this is the first version that was printed in English.

Geneva Bible–1560

This version is the work of William Whittingham, who was the first to use the verse and chapter divisions found in our modern-day Bibles. He did his work with a group of English exiles living in Geneva, Switzerland. The Geneva Bible was also the first Bible to contain extensive study notes and was a favorite of the Puritans.

The King James Version–1611

After King Henry VIII severed his country's ties with the Catholic Church, a need arose for an English version of the Bible that could be used in the Protestant churches. On July 22, 1604, King James I announced that he had appointed 54 men as translators, the only qualification being that they should be "proficient as Bible scholars." The translation work was the most thorough ever done up to that date. Six different groups of scholars would first translate a given section of the Scripture, and then their translation was examined by the five other groups. A committee of six was selected from all the translators to be the final authority in translation matters.

The King James Version stood for many years in a class by itself. Its smooth-flowing older-style language, based heavily on Wycliffe's 1382 version, gave it a majestic note not shared by any other translation up to that time. Up through the latter half of the twentieth century, it was the most popular English Bible version available. We do not possess the actual manuscripts from which the King James Version was translated, but the ancient manuscripts that have been discovered since 1611 verify its accuracy and reliability.

The American Standard Version–1901

This Bible is a revision of the English Revised Version of 1895, which was a very thorough translation itself. The ASV is regarded by conservative Bible scholars as the most reliable and best translation available today. Since its translation it has been updated and retitled the New American Standard Bible, and it is the version many Greek scholars choose because they believe it comes the closest to the original languages.

Many Modern Translations–1950 to Today

The last half of the twentieth century saw such a proliferation of English translations that there are too many to mention here—including the New King James Version (NKJV), the New International Version (NIV), and the English Standard Version (ESV). Numerous other translations and paraphrases have added to the many millions of Bibles that are printed every year. In addition to the many English translations, the Bible has been translated into more than 2000 languages, including all the major languages of the world: Spanish, French, Russian, German, Portuguese, Chinese, Japanese, Hindi, and Arabic, thus making the Word of God available worldwide.

CREATION WEEK

THE BIBLE SAYS IN GENESIS 1:1, "In the beginning God created the heavens and the earth." These seven words in the Hebrew text are the title of the opening book of Scripture and summarize everything that is unfolded step by step in the following verses. The second verse provides three circumstantial clauses, setting the stage for the days of creation that follow in verse 3. These clauses state the condition of the earth as it was when created out of nothing. The first clause says, "The earth was formless and void." Second, we are told that "darkness was over the surface of the deep." And third, "the Spirit of God was moving over the surface of the waters." These three statements describe the circumstances present as God began the creation week of seven literal days.

Genesis 1:3 is the main clause describing the first act in forming the present universe. Thus, there is no basis in the text, nor any reason from the context, to see a gap or period of time between Genesis 1:1 and 1:2. The creation of the universe is described as God speaking the world into existence *ex nihilo* (from nothing). It is pictured as an instantaneous appearance of matter from which the world was constructed, rather than an unformed mass left from the judgment of a prior world.

God formed His creation during the first three days of creation week and filled it on the second three days. On day one God made light and called it day. The darkness He called night, and He separated the light from darkness (Genesis 1:3-5). On day two God separated the waters above from the waters below, with the sky in between (Genesis 1:6-8). He called the sky heaven. On day three God separated dry land from the waters below (Genesis 1:9-13). He called the land earth and also made every kind of plant.

The seven days of creation week are divided into three segments. The first three days correct the condition of "formlessness," while the next three days fill the "void" condition mentioned in verse 2. Then on the seventh day, God rested from His creation work of the previous six days and declared that His handiwork was very good (Genesis 1:31–2:3). The creation was deemed very good because God had formed it and filled it. What God had done would be similar to a person building a house and then stocking it with all the needed furnishings.

After the first three days had passed, God spent the next three "filling" His creation. On day four He made the luminaries to fill the sky: the sun for the day, the moon for the night, and the stars in the

The Creation Week
(Genesis 1)

Day One	Day Two	Day Three	Day Four	Day Five	Day Six	Day Seven
divide light from darkness	divide upper waters from expanse lower waters	divide lower waters from dry land	to fill the luminaries: sun, moon, and stars	to fill the earth: fish and birds	to fill the earth: beasts and man	God ceases creation and rests from His work
FORMLESS To correct the "without form" condition, three acts of "dividing"			VOID To correct the "void" condition, three acts of "furnishing"			REST

sky (Genesis 1:14–19). The luminaries were also given for signs, seasons, days, and years. Some speculate that the angelic realm was also created on the fourth day because Genesis 1:16 concludes with "He made the stars also." It is observed that throughout Scripture, there is a relationship between the physical stars and angels. If so, then this explains why the "morning stars" (angels) were able to sing for joy at the conclusion of the creation week (Job 38:7). On day five God filled the sea with fish and other creatures and the air with birds (Genesis 1:20-23). On day six He made land animals, reptiles, insects, and finally, one man and one woman (Genesis 1:24-31). God mandated that humanity was to multiply, subdue the earth, and rule over it (Genesis 1:28).

God's workweek ended after the sixth day, and He rested on the seventh (Genesis 2:1-3). He did not rest because He was tired, for it is impossible for Him to get tired. Instead, He rested on the seventh day because He had completed all that He had purposed to do, and this perfectly functioning universe was said to be especially good. This means that whatever God did to create the original universe is no longer in operation in the manner in which it was at that time. However, God never rests from sovereignly ruling and sustaining His creation.

TIMELINE OF ELECT AND FALLEN ANGELS

A FIXED NUMBER OF ANGELS were created—possibly on the fourth day of creation—and sang for joy when they witnessed God's completed creation (Job 38:7). In the Bible, there are almost 400 references to angels. We know that God created millions of them (Hebrews 12:22; Revelation 5:11), and in Scripture, we see them referred to as male in gender.

Angels were given great power both in the spiritual and physical realms. They were also created as mature beings—they do not age, nor have there ever been baby angels or old angels. We also know that angels cannot die. And it's clear that they possess great power both in the spiritual and physical realms.

Scripture classifies angels as either holy or unfallen (Mark 8:38) and fallen (Matthew 25:41), also known as demons (Mark 5:15). The fallen angels can never be saved and redeemed as a human can by trusting in Christ as their Savior. Also, because God created the angelic population in a moment of time, they lack the genealogical solidarity found in humanity. This is in contrast to humanity—every human being literally descends from Adam, including Eve, who was taken from the side of Adam. Thus, all humanity has the DNA of Adam and is savable, because Jesus came to earth and partook of Adam's humanity in order to identify as a human. This made the human race savable (Hebrews 2:14).

Revelation 12:4,9 tells us that a third of the angels fell and followed Lucifer in their rebellion against God. Eventually, these fallen angels will be cast into the Lake of Fire and spend eternity there (Matthew 25:41). The other two-thirds of the angels continue to serve God and follow His plan for them. Their destinies appear locked in place for all eternity, and it does not appear that they will ever be tested again at a future time.

The Bible makes it clear that angels are created beings and came into existence at the creation. "For by Him [Jesus Christ] all things were created, both in the heavens and on earth, visible and invisible, whether thrones or dominions or rulers or authorities—all things have been created through Him and for Him" (Colossians 1:16). The writer of Hebrews, quoting Psalm 104, said, "Of the angels He says, 'Who make His angels winds, and His ministers a flame of fire'" (Hebrews

Timeline of Elect and Fallen Angels

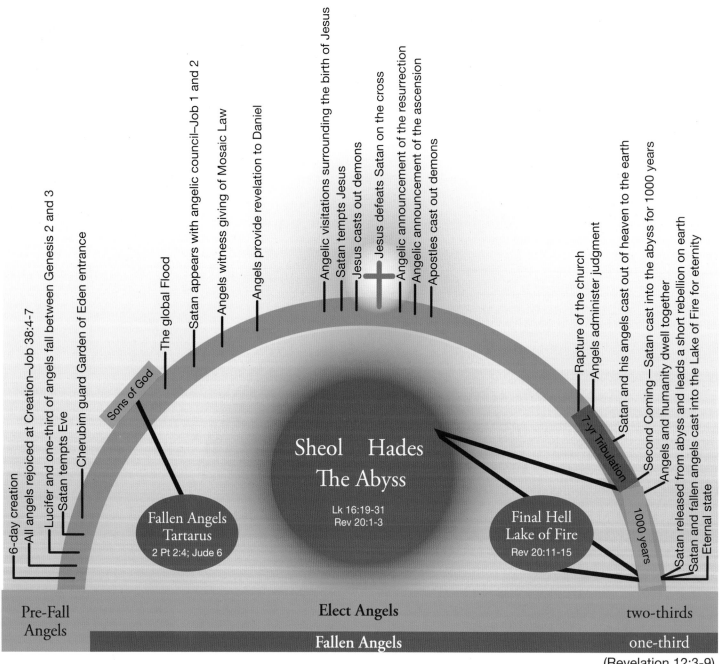

6-day creation

All angels rejoiced at Creation–Job 38:4-7

Lucifer and one-third of angels fall between Genesis 2 and 3

Satan tempts Eve

Cherubim guard Garden of Eden entrance

Sons of God

The global Flood

Satan appears with angelic council–Job 1 and 2

Angels witness giving of Mosaic Law

Angels provide revelation to Daniel

Angelic visitations surrounding the birth of Jesus

Satan tempts Jesus

Jesus casts out demons

Jesus defeats Satan on the cross

Angelic announcement of the resurrection

Angelic announcement of the ascension

Apostles cast out demons

Rapture of the church

Angels administer judgment

Satan and his angels cast out of heaven to the earth

Second Coming—Satan cast into the abyss for 1000 years

Angels and humanity dwell together

Satan released from abyss and leads a short rebellion on earth

Satan and fallen angels cast into the Lake of Fire for eternity

7-yr Tribulation

1000 years

Eternal state

Sheol   Hades
The Abyss

Lk 16:19-31
Rev 20:1-3

Fallen Angels
Tartarus

2 Pt 2:4; Jude 6

Final Hell
Lake of Fire

Rev 20:11-15

Pre-Fall
Angels

Elect Angels

two-thirds

Fallen Angels

one-third

(Revelation 12:3-9)

1:7). Thus, angels were created to act as God's ministering agents and messengers (which is the meaning of the word *angel* in the original Hebrew and Greek texts of Scripture).

There was a great amount of visible angelic activity among humans before the Flood, and there will be great activity during the Tribulation, second coming, and also the millennial kingdom. The current church age is a time of behind-the-scenes angelic activity from both the elect and fallen angels. For example, we are told by the apostle Paul, "Put on the full armor of God, that you will be able to stand firm against the schemes of the devil. For our struggle is not against flesh and blood, but against the rulers, against the powers, against the world forces of this darkness, against the spiritual forces of wickedness in the heavenly places" (Ephesians 6:11-12).

Scripture indicates that for now, humanity is "a little lower" than the angels (Psalm 8:5). In the future, church-age believers are destined to rule over angels: "Do you not know that the saints will judge the world? And if the world is judged by you, are you not competent to constitute the smallest law courts? Do you not know that we will judge angels? How much more matters of this life" (1 Corinthians 6:2-3). The church's future rule over angels is one reason the elect angels are watching what is going on in the church's assemblies (1 Corinthians 11:10).

During the Tribulation, God will use angels—both elect and fallen—as instruments of His wrath upon a sinful world. For example, He will use elect angels to administer the trumpet judgments of Revelation 8 and 9. And He will use fallen angels, or demons, as His agents of wrath in the fifth and sixth trumpet judgments.

Scripture clearly teaches there is coming a day when Satan and his demonic agents will be judged and all their influence will be removed from the earth. They will be cast into the Lake of Fire (Matthew 25:41; Revelation 20:10). After that, God will totally destroy the present heavens and earth (2 Peter 3:10-12) and replace them with the brand new heavens and earth (2 Peter 3:13; Revelation 21:1). Because evil in all its forms will have been forever confined to the Lake of Fire, it will never be present in the new heavens and new earth. Thus, both elect angels and saved mankind will no longer be tested. Redeemed humanity and the elect angels will spend all eternity serving and praising God without sin natures within and with no evil or curse in the new environment. From then onward, both angels and humans will experience nothing but eternal bliss in the presence of the Triune God and His creation.

5

THE DIVINE INSTITUTIONS

S WE SEE THE DECLINE of the remnants of a Christian-based culture in the United States and throughout the world, we need to be reminded of God's standards and purpose for humanity. God's will for mankind was revealed in the first book of the Bible—Genesis. Learning about the divine institutions provides a summary framework for understanding what God desires for His creation. The divine institutions function within the biblical covenants that relate to mankind's social life. Charles Clough observes that "divine institutions are real absolute structures built into man's social existence."[1] According to him, "The term 'divine institution' has been used for centuries by Christians, particularly in Reformed circles, to describe the fixed, basic social forms."[2]

Divine institutions were created by God and are sourced in the divine, but they apply to all mankind from the time of Adam and Eve. Man's basic social structures did not just evolve over time, but were built into God's creation.

Pre-Fall Divine Institutions

The first divine institution is *responsible dominion* (Genesis 1:26-30; 2:15-17; Psalm 8:3-8). It is the sphere in which an individual is responsible to God for the decisions he makes. Man was created to be God's vice-regent over planet Earth in order to manage it under God's authority. The Fall resulted in a perversion of man's responsibility, but that responsibility was never taken away.[3] This means that each human being is responsible before God for creative labor that was intended to glorify God. God designed it so that through individual choices, we may demonstrate either a record of obedience to or rebellion against the Creator. Clough makes this observation about mankind after the Fall: "Instead of peaceable, godly dominion over all the earth under God and His Word, man fights and claws his way to a counterfeit dominion built of his own works (cf. Jas 4:1-4)."[4] Individual choice is the area in which a person is responsible to either trust

Christ as their Savior or reject Him. No one else can make that choice on behalf of another.

The second divine institution is *marriage* (Genesis 2:18-24). This institution is deduced from the original marriage of Adam and Eve in Genesis 2. It is within this realm that sexual relations are to be experienced, and together, the husband and wife are to fulfill the cultural mandate to rule over the creation. We see that the woman is called a "helper" who was brought by God to Adam, who needed a helper corresponding to himself to aid him in his calling to rule over creation. "Unlike animals, mankind's so-called sexual differentiation is not merely for procreation; it is also for dominion."[5] "Later the extreme importance of the structure of marriage appears in the NT when Paul reveals that it typifies the union between Christ and the Church (Eph. 5:22-33)."[6] Clough explains:

> Mankind cannot express God's image except as both "male and female" together (Genesis 1:27). This is because God has certain characteristics that are "feminine" in nature (e.g., Matthew 23:37). Moreover, the woman's role as "helper" in Genesis 2:18 is not meant to be a demeaning, secondary one. The term used for "helper" elsewhere is used of God Himself (Exod. 18:4; Deuteronomy 33:7)…
>
> Undeniably, however, the Bible places emphasis upon the man as the one who receives his calling from God which then shapes his choice of wife…Together in a division of labor man and wife separate from their own family, in contrast to an extended family, does a young man have to face full leadership responsibility directly under God.[7]

The third divine institution is built upon the first two and is that of *family*. "In the Bible it is the family, not the individual, that is the basic unit of society (property, for example, is titled under the Mosaic law to families)."[8] "Family exists for training of the next generation (cf. Exod. 20:12; Deuteronomy 6:4-9; Eph. 6:1-4)."[9] Family is the institution responsible for continuing each family legacy by being responsible for education and wealth. Even if a family chooses to use surrogate teachers, it is still responsible for seeing that a child is properly educated. Clough tells us:

> Family and marriage cannot be separated from dominion. Where dominion is perverted and the environment ruined, starvation and poverty follow. Where marriage is dishonored and where families are broken, society collapses. No amount of laws, programs, or "redefinitions" of marriage and family can save the day. God designed the divine institutions to provide dominion and prosperity.[10]

The Fall did not change any of the divine institutions. Instead, it corrupted man, who misuses them. Clough notes:

> When faced with the corruption in each of these social structures, fallen man responds in several ways. One way is to reinterpret the struggles with sin in terms of economics (Marx's "class war") or of race (white and black racists) or of psychology (Freud and others). Another cop-out is to abandon the institutions themselves as outdated, arbitrary social "conventions" that need "re-engineering." All such responses, however, are costly failures to the societies that try them. In the end, they reflect the pagan mindset that denies the responsibility of the fall and the abnormality of evil.[11]

Post-Fall Divine Institutions

At least two more divine institutions were established after the Fall. Both were instituted after the Flood and were designed to restrain evil in a fallen world. The first three divine institutions, or pre-Fall institutions (responsible dominion, marriage, and family) are the positive or productive ones of society. The next two, the post-Fall, are negative because their intent is to restrain evil.

Of the post-Fall institutions, the first one (or the fourth divine institution overall) is *civil government*, whereby God transferred to man, through the Noahic Covenant, the responsibility to exercise civil

The Divine Institutions

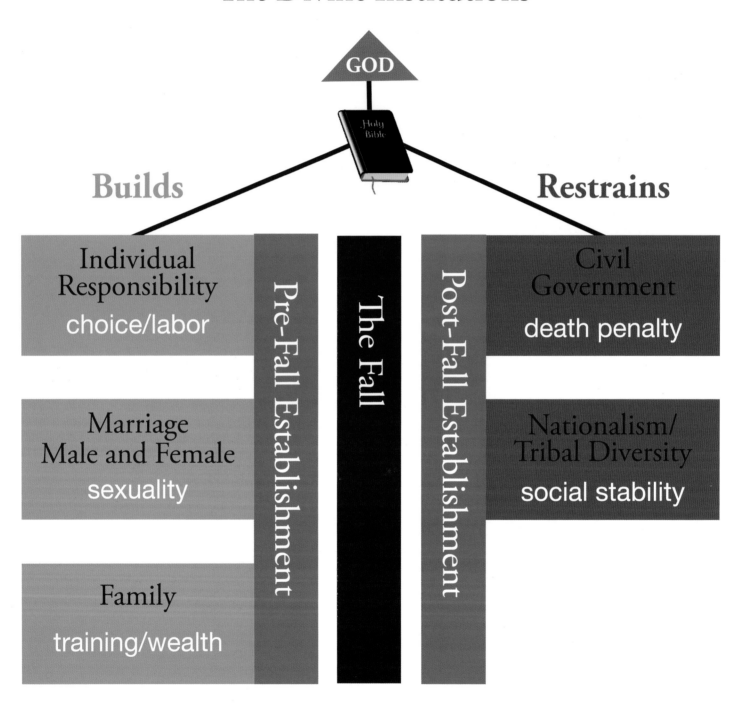

GOD

Holy Bible

Builds

Restrains

Individual
Responsibility
choice/labor

Pre-Fall Establishment

The Fall

Post-Fall Establishment

Civil
Government
death penalty

Marriage
Male and Female
sexuality

Nationalism/
Tribal Diversity
social stability

Family
training/wealth

authority for the purpose of restraining evil after the Flood (Genesis 9:5-6). Before the Flood, man could not execute judgment upon evil as seen in the way in which God commanded man to deal with Cain's murder of Abel (Genesis 4:9-15). This divine institution is based upon capital punishment (Genesis 9:5-6) and, as said earlier, is for the purpose of restraining evil (Romans 13:3-4). Lesser judicial authority is implied in the God-given command for civil institutions to exact a life for life. Even though capital punishment has grown distasteful to apostate Western culture, it is still the basis for God's establishment of civil government.[12]

The second post-Fall institution (or the fifth divine institution overall) is *tribal diversity* or *nationalism*, which was also established after the Flood to help promote social stability in a fallen world (see Genesis 9:25-27, and compare with Genesis 10–11 and Deuteronomy 32:8). Notice this is not racial diversity, but tribal diversity. This divine institution does not involve race but tribes or families.

Tribal diversity was implemented through the confusion of languages at the Tower of Babel (Genesis 11:1-9). Why did God want to separate people in this fashion? Many believe mankind should come together in unity. Genesis 11:6 explains why God confused human language: "The LORD said, 'Behold, they are one people, and they all have the same language. And this is what they began to do, and now nothing which they purpose to do will be impossible for them.'" The reason humanity wanted to unite itself was to more effectively rebel against God, as seen in the Tower of Babel incident. This explains why people today are moving more and more toward globalism (at the same time they are moving further away from God). As Scripture says, during the Tribulation, the Antichrist will forge together a one-world government set against the plan and purposes of God. The Tribulation will end with God's direct intervention and judgment, as at the Flood. In the meantime, God slows down man's collective rebellion through civil government and tribal diversity.

Implications

In review, then, we see that this biblical approach to government and society is consistent with the theological principles of dispensationalism (for an expanded definition of dispensationalism, see chapter 9). These responsibilities were given through the divine institutions to all mankind either at Creation or after the Flood. This understanding produces a conservative view of government and looks to individual responsibility, marriage, and the family as the productive sectors in a society. Because civil government's primary responsibility is to restrain evil so that the pre-Fall institutions can be productive, we can know that the Bible does not support any form of government planning or interference in those productive institutions. During the current church age, then, an individual believer should function socially within the framework of the divine institutions while taking into account whatever commands are given to him as a member of the church, the body of Christ.

6

PRE-FLOOD GENEALOGY

THE FIRST OF 39 BIBLICAL GENEALOGIES appears in Genesis chapter 5. One feature that makes this genealogy distinctive is that, when compared to other biblical genealogies, it is one of only two (the other is in Genesis 11) that provides numbers that make it possible for one to count and come up with a related chronology for the pre-Flood era. In fact, not only does Genesis 5 provide a sequence of life spans that enables one to compile a chronological time line from Creation to the Flood, it also provides the data for figuring out the time span using an alternate approach. Both approaches come up with the same exact number of years between Creation and the Flood, which is 1656 years. This supports the notion that one of God's intents in Genesis 5 was to provide mankind with a chronological framework from Creation to the Flood.

The days and years of the pre-Flood world were very similar to the days and years we experience now. There is no reason to think the days of the pre-Flood world were any different chronologically than our current 24-hour day. We can see from Genesis 6 through 8 a detailed account of Noah's life for one year. Genesis 7:11 says, "In the six hundredth year of Noah's life, in the second month, on the seventeenth day of the month, on the same day," the Flood began. Genesis 8:3-4 tells us Noah's age when the ark came to rest upon the mountains of Ararat, which was 600 years, 7 months, and 17 days old. Genesis 8:3 tells us that 150 days passed from the time the Flood event began—when Noah was 600 years, 2 months, and 17 days old—till the time the Ark rested on Ararat, when Noah was 600 years, 7 months, and 17 days old. Thus, 5 months had gone by (150 days divided by 5 months equals a 30-day month). Therefore, it is clear that 12 months (or one year) equals 360 days in a year. Our solar year today is 365¼ days per year, so the earth's rotational cycle must have slowed down a little at some point in history.

Two Ways to Calculate Genealogy

The first way to calculate the genealogies is to add the span of time between the birth of a patriarch and the birth of his son in the stated line of descent. The second way is to determine Adam's age when Methuselah was born (since Methuselah died in the year in which the

Flood occurred), then add Methuselah's life span to Adam's age at his birth. This yields the same number of years as the first approach. This means that we are dealing with real numbers and that there are no chronological gaps in the Genesis 5 genealogy, even though the patriarchs listed in the genealogies had other sons and daughters. Thus, a total of 1656 years passed from Creation to the Flood.

First Approach

Patriarch	Time Span	Running Total
Adam		
Seth	130	130
Enosh	105	235
Kenan	90	325
Mahalalel	70	395
Jared	65	460
Enoch	162	622
Methuselah	65	687
Lamech	187	874
Noah	182	1056
Shem	502	1558
Shem's age at Flood (Genesis 11:10)	98	1656

Second Approach

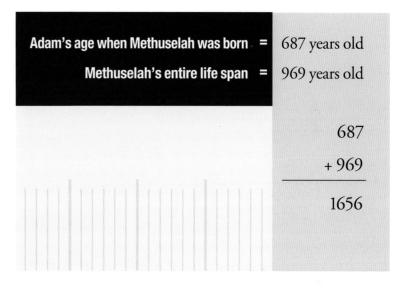

Adam's age when Methuselah was born	=	687 years old
Methuselah's entire life span	=	969 years old

$$687$$
$$+ \ 969$$
$$\overline{1656}$$

When taken together with all the other chronological data, it seems apparent that the current age of the earth is just about two decades more than 6000 years old. Such a viewpoint appears to be the logical conclusion from the biblical data. Obviously a young earth model makes sense when compared to the billions of years for the age of the heavens and earth believed by those who reject God's account recorded in the Bible.

Pre-Flood Genealogy
(Genesis 5)

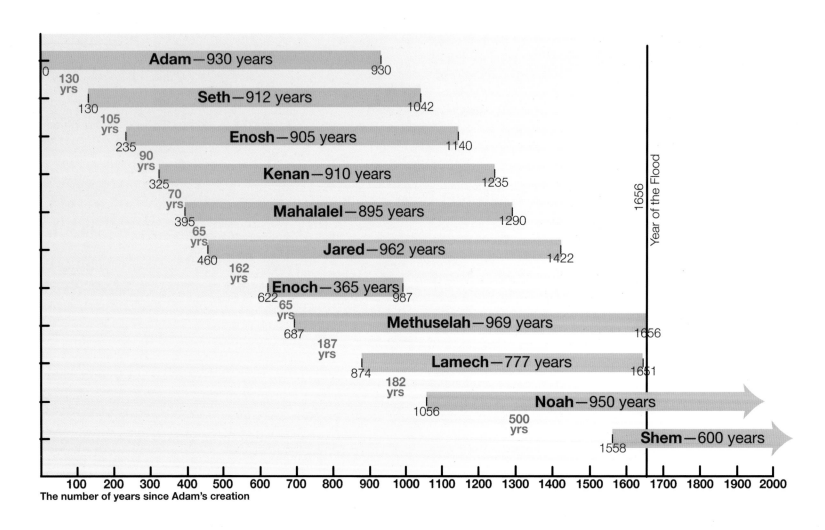

Adam—930 years
0
930

130 yrs
Seth—912 years
130
1042

105 yrs
Enosh—905 years
235
1140

90 yrs
Kenan—910 years
325
1235

70 yrs
Mahalalel—895 years
395
1290

65 yrs
Jared—962 years
460
1422

162 yrs
Enoch—365 years
622
987

65 yrs
Methuselah—969 years
687
1656

187 yrs
Lamech—777 years
874
1651

182 yrs
Noah—950 years
1056

500 yrs
Shem—600 years
1558

Year of the Flood — 1656

100 200 300 400 500 600 700 800 900 1000 1100 1200 1300 1400 1500 1600 1700 1800 1900 2000

The number of years since Adam's creation

THE COVENANTS

GOD'S RELATIONSHIP WITH MAN is always mediated through one or more of the biblical covenants. God has made promises in history and has bound Himself by covenants to guarantee that He will fulfill His promises. The God who cannot lie, nevertheless, binds Himself with covenants that further guarantee that He will keep His word.

What is the nature of the biblical covenants? First, covenants are contracts between individuals for the purpose of governing a relationship. God has willingly bound Himself to His people to keep His promises so He can demonstrate, over the course of history, what kind of God He is. Second, relationships in the Bible, especially between God and man, are legal or judicial. This is why relational interaction between God and mankind are mediated through covenants. Covenants usually involve intent, promises, and sanctions.

Kinds of Covenants

There are three kinds of covenants in Scripture:

Royal Grant Treaty (unconditional)

A promissory covenant that arose out of a king's desire to reward a loyal servant.

Examples:

The Abrahamic Covenant

The Davidic Covenant

The Royal Grant treaties or covenants are unconditional. This fact is important because at stake is whether or not God is obligated to fulfill His promise specifically to the original parties of the covenant. For example, we believe that God must fulfill to Israel—as a national entity—those promises made to them through unconditional covenants like the Abrahamic, Davidic, and the Land of Israel covenant. If this is true, then they must be fulfilled literally, and that means many aspects are yet future. Dr. Arnold Fruchtenbaum has said:

An unconditional covenant can be defined as a sovereign act of God whereby God unconditionally obligates Himself

The Biblical Covenants

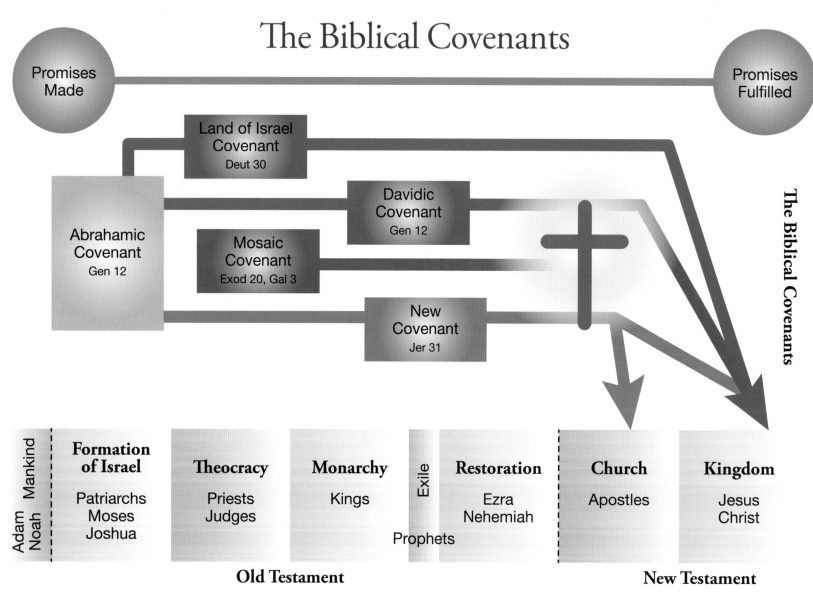

Adapted from Paul Benware, *Understanding End Times Prophecy: A Comprehensive Approach* (Chicago: Moody Press, 1995), 50.

to bring to pass definite promises, blessings, and conditions for the covenanted people. It is a unilateral covenant. This type of covenant is characterized by the formula I will which declares God's determination to do exactly as He promised. The blessings are secured by the grace of God.[1]

Suzerain-Vassal Treaty (conditional)

This bound an inferior vassal to a superior suzerain and was binding only on the one who swore.

Examples:

Chedorlaomer (Genesis 14)

Jabesh-Gilead serving Nahash (1 Samuel 11:1)

The Mosaic Covenant (Book of Deuteronomy)

This covenantal arrangement is important because the stipulations are conditional and based upon whether or not the vassal adheres to the stipulations of the agreement. Therefore, unlike the Royal Grant, which is unconditional, the Suzerain-Vassal Treaty rewards or curses the vassal based upon whether the individual keeps or disobeys the stipulations that are stated in the covenant.

Parity Treaty

This bound two equal parties in a relationship and provided conditions as stipulated by the participants.

Examples:

Abraham and Abimelech (Genesis 21:25-32)

Jacob and Laban (Genesis 31:44-50)

David and Jonathan (1 Samuel 18:1-4; cf. 2 Samuel 9:1-13)

Christ and church-age believers; i.e., "friends" (John 15)

The Covenants Found in the Bible

In the Bible, there are at least eight covenants between God and people:

The Edenic Covenant (Genesis 1:28-30; 2:15-17)

In the Edenic Covenant, which was stated before the Fall, God established His rule and relationship to mankind. The Edenic Covenant, in conjunction with the Cultural Mandate (Genesis 1:26-28), provided the basis for human responsibility, social, political, and economic duties; and accountability before God. After the fall into sin, other covenants augmented this foundational relationship.

The Adamic Covenant (Genesis 3:14-19)

God initiated this covenant because of Adam's sin. This covenant acknowledges the cursed status of man and creation that all must endure throughout history. The curse will be removed primarily during the millennial reign of Christ (Romans 8:19-23), and death will be eliminated altogether in the eternal state (1 Corinthians 15:53-57; Revelation 21:4; 22:3).

The Noahic Covenant (Genesis 8:20–9:17)

The Noahic Covenant restated God's authority over man and his duties as found in the Adamic Covenant (Genesis 9:1), and then added further responsibilities. These additions included the following: (1) Animosity between mankind and the animal kingdom (9:2); (2) man could now eat animal flesh for food (9:3); (3) while eating flesh, the blood will not be consumed, but drained (9:4); (4) human life is so valuable that God requires the death of the one who murders another—capital punishment (9:5-6); (5) and the command, "Be fruitful and multiply, and fill the earth" (Genesis 9:1,7). The Noahic Covenant was a contract between God and all subsequent humanity, including the entire animal kingdom (9:8-10). In this covenant, God promised to never again destroy the world through a flood (9:11). The sign that God would keep His promise was a rainbow set within a cloud (9:12-17). It is possible God chose to use a rainbow because that is what surrounds the very throne room of God (Ezekiel 1:28; Revelation 4:3), representing His person and presence. The Noahic Covenant is clearly stated in Isaiah 54:9-10.

The Abrahamic Covenant
(Genesis 12:1-3; 15:1-21)

The Abrahamic Covenant is the mother of all redemptive covenants. Every blessing experienced by the redeemed, both within Israel and the church, flows from this covenant. While the covenant was first introduced in Genesis 12:1-3, it was declared in Genesis 15:1-21, reaffirmed in Genesis 17:1-21, and then renewed with Isaac in Genesis 26:2-5 and Jacob in Genesis 28:10-17. It is a covenant in which God unconditionally obligates Himself to bring to pass definite promises, blessings, and conditions for His covenanted people.

The three major provisions of the Abrahamic Covenant were (1) land to Abram, Israel, and Abram's physical descendants; (2) a seed (including Christ); (3) a worldwide blessing. The Abrahamic Covenant is directed to Abraham, Isaac, Jacob, and their descendants. It is repeated to them 20 times in Genesis (12:1-3,7-9; 13:14-18; 15:1-18; 17:1-27; 22:15-19; 26:2-6,24-25; 27:28-29,38-40; 28:1-4,10-22; 31:3,11-13; 32:22-32; 35:9-15; 48:3-4,10-20; 49:1-28; 50:23-25). In all, the Abrahamic Covenant includes more than a dozen provisions. Some apply to Abraham; some to Israel, the seed; and some pertain to Gentiles.

The Mosaic Covenant
(Exodus 20–23; Deuteronomy)

The Mosaic Covenant was given exclusively to the nation of Israel (Psalm 147:19-20) and was fulfilled through the ministry of Jesus Christ during His first advent (Matthew 5:17). The Mosaic Covenant is a conditional covenant that was designed to teach Israel how to please God as His chosen nation. The measuring stick was to be the Law aspect of the Covenant. The Law was designed to govern every aspect of Israel's life: the spiritual, moral, social, religious, and civil aspects. The commandments were a "ministry of condemnation" and "of death" (2 Corinthians 3:7-9). The church-age believer is not in any way, shape, or form under the obligations of the Mosaic Law, but under the unconditional Law of Christ and the Spirit (Romans 3:21-27; 6:14-15; Galatians 2:16; 3:10,16-18,24-26; 4:21-31; Hebrews

10:11-17). The Mosaic Covenant did not change the provision of the Abrahamic Covenant, but was an addendum for a limited time only—until Christ came (Galatians 3:17-19).

The Davidic Covenant (2 Samuel 7:4-17)

The Davidic Covenant is the foundation upon which the future millennial kingdom of the Lord Jesus Christ will be founded. It promised to David (1) posterity in the Davidic house; (2) a throne symbolic of royal authority; (3) a kingdom, or rule on earth; and (4) certainty of fulfillment of the promises made to David.

Solomon, whose birth God predicted (2 Samuel 7:12), was not promised a perpetual seed, but only assured that (1) he would build "a house for God" (2 Samuel 7:13); (2) his kingdom would be established (2 Samuel 7:12); (3) his throne, or royal authority, would endure forever; and (4) if Solomon sinned, he would be chastised but not deposed. The continuation of Solomon's throne, but not his seed, shows the accuracy of the prediction. Most of these promises will be fulfilled during the millennial reign of Christ.

The Land of Israel Covenant
(Deuteronomy 30:1-10)

This covenant provided an expansion upon the land promise found in the Abrahamic Covenant (Genesis 12:1-3). In Deuteronomy, after two chapters that predicted disobedience and judgment and deportation from the land, the Lord foretold of ultimate repentance and blessing upon national Israel. He bound Himself to this ultimate destiny for Israel by establishing a covenant that promised the land to Israel forever.

This covenant unfolds as follows: (1) dispersion for disobedience (Deuteronomy 30:1; see also Deuteronomy 28:63-68; 29:22-28); (2) the future repentance of Israel while in dispersion (Deuteronomy 30:2; see also Deuteronomy 28:63-68); (3) the Messiah will gather the remaining exiles and transport them to the land (Deuteronomy 30:3-6; see also Daniel 12:1; Zechariah 2:6; Amos 9:14; Matthew 24:31); (4) the land will be permanently restored to Israel

(Deuteronomy 30:5; see also Isaiah 11:11-12; Jeremiah 23:3-8; Ezekiel 37:21-25); (5) the whole nation of Israel will be converted to their Messiah (Deuteronomy 30:6; see also Hosea 2:14-16; Zechariah 12:10-14; Romans 11:26-27); (6) judgment of those who oppose Israel (Deuteronomy 30:7; see also Isaiah 14:1-2; Joel 3:1-8; Matthew 25:31-46); and (7) Israel will experience national blessing and prosperity (Deuteronomy 30:9; see also Amos 9:11-15; Zechariah 14:9-21).

The New Covenant
(Jeremiah 31:31-37 and other passages)

The New Covenant provides for the yet-future spiritual regeneration of Israel in preparation for the millennial kingdom. The New Covenant, as stated here and in other Old Testament passages, is for Israel (Deuteronomy 29:4; 30:6; Isaiah 59:20-21; 61:8-9; Jeremiah 32:37-40; 50:4-5; Ezekiel 11:19-20; 16:60-63; 37:21-28; 34:25-26; 36:24-27; Zechariah 9:11; 12:10; Hebrews 8:1-13; 10:15-18). The New Covenant is applied to the church (Matthew 26:27-28; Luke 22:20; 2 Corinthians 3:6) because it provides the forgiveness of sins and a spiritual dynamic that is not reserved solely for the nation of Israel.

All of these covenants were made early in the history of mankind or at the beginning of the founding of the nation of Israel. Jesus the Messiah will be the basis for the fulfillment, in history, of all these covenants. In fact, Paul states that all the covenants belong to Israel (Romans 9:4). There are no covenants made with the church. Church-age believers gain their standing and receive the forgiveness of sin through believing in Christ, who then adopts them into His family. They receive the benefits of the covenants that relate to salvation from sin through their adoption by Christ. Christ is the central figure within the covenantal framework of Scripture, and most look forward to a future, final fulfillment in relation to Israel. Some of the *spiritual* benefits of the covenants are applied by Christ to believers in the present church age through their adoption into Christ.

THE BIBLICAL AND HISTORICAL account of Noah and the Flood began at least 120 years before the Flood itself, with God speaking to Noah and telling him to build an ark: "Then the LORD said, 'My Spirit shall not strive with man forever, because he also is flesh; nevertheless his days shall be one hundred and twenty years'" (Genesis 6:3). Noah was then called to build the ark, which would save him and his family—a total of eight people. "Make for yourself an ark of gopher wood" (Genesis 6:14). Thus Noah—and presumably his family—began work on the ark 120 years before the Flood.

Noah and his family were in the ark a little longer than a year. Genesis 7:11-13 tells us Noah entered the ark when he was 600 years, 2 months, and 17 days old. We learn in Genesis 8:14-15 that Noah left the ark a year and 10 days after entering it. Therefore, Noah and his family were in the ark for a total of 371 days.

Some have thought Noah was in the ark for only 40 days and nights. Genesis (7:4,12,17) notes that it rained at the beginning of the Flood for 40 days and nights. Scripture then says: "The water prevailed and increased greatly upon the earth; and the ark floated on the surface of the water. And the water prevailed more and more upon the earth, so that all the high mountains everywhere under the heavens were covered. The water prevailed fifteen cubits higher, and the mountains were covered" (Genesis 7:18-20). A few verses later we learn that "the water prevailed upon the earth one hundred and fifty days" (Genesis 7:24). It took the rest of the year for the water to dissipate enough for Noah and his family to come out onto dry land.

Seven days before Noah entered the ark, the Lord said, "After seven more days, I will send rain on the earth forty days and forty nights; and I will blot out from the face of the land every living thing that I have made" (Genesis 7:4). After the seven-day preparation and the gathering of the animals the Lord sent the Flood (Genesis 7:10). It's noteworthy that Noah did not close the door to the ark; rather, Scripture says of the ark's door, "the LORD closed it behind him [Noah]" (Genesis 7:16).

On that day when Noah went into the ark, the rain began and the fountains of the deep broke open. It rained for 40 days and nights (Genesis 7:4,11-12,17). After the 40 days of rain, we read that "the water prevailed and increased greatly...so that all the high mountains everywhere under the heavens were covered" (Genesis 7:18-19). The water "prevailed upon the earth one hundred and fifty days" (Genesis 7:24). This means that during the 150-day period, the water came during the first 40 days, and from then onward, the "water prevailed fifteen cubits higher, and the mountains were covered" (Genesis 7:20). Thus, the highest mountain and the rest of planet's land mass were at least 20 feet under water for a total of 110 days. This resulted in the death of all living things.

Chronology of the Flood
(Genesis 7–8)

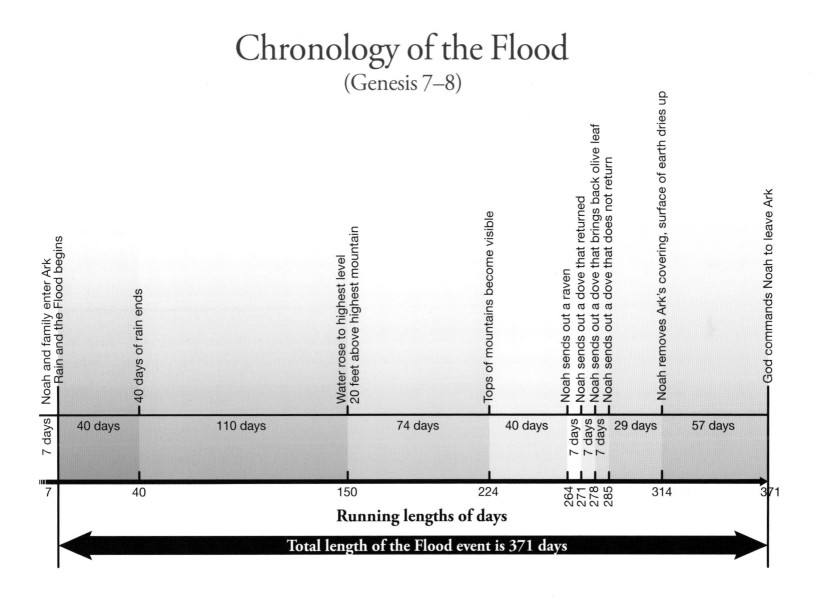

Running lengths of days

Total length of the Flood event is 371 days

All flesh that moved on the earth perished, birds and cattle and beasts and every swarming thing that swarms upon the earth, and all mankind; of all that was on the dry land, all in whose nostrils was the breath of the spirit of life, died. Thus He blotted out every living thing that was upon the face of the land, from man to animals to creeping things and to birds of the sky, and they were blotted out from the earth; and only Noah was left, together with those that were with him in the ark (Genesis 7:21-23).

Fish and other sea creatures are not mentioned as being destroyed in the Flood, so we assume that they transitioned from the old world to the new through the water.

"The water decreased steadily until the tenth month; in the tenth month, on the first day of the month, the tops of the mountains became visible" (Genesis 8:5). The waters began to decrease after the first 150 days of the Flood, and after 74 days of decline, the tops of mountains became visible to Noah. After another 40 days, Noah opened the window of the ark and sent out a raven, which did not return to the ark (Genesis 8:6-7). Seven days later a dove was sent out. Because it could not find a resting place, it returned to the ark (Genesis 8:8-9). After another seven-day wait, Noah sent out the dove again, and this time she returned with an olive leaf (Genesis 8:10-11). After yet another seven days, the dove was sent out again, and this time she did not return at all (Genesis 8:12).

Twenty-nine days later, Noah removed the covering of the ark and saw dry land (Genesis 8:13). The text says, "And in the second month, on the twenty-seventh day of the month, the earth was dry" (Genesis 8:14). Yet Noah stayed in the ark another 57 days until God told him, "Go out of the ark, you and your wife and your sons and your sons' wives with you" (Genesis 8:16).

As is the case with the entire Bible, these early chapters of Genesis are dealing with real history that took place in actual space and time, and these events have been accurately revealed to us by God Himself. The Flood and what happened afterward was a sequence of events that really took place over a 371-day period of time.

9

THE DISPENSATIONS

ISPENSATIONALISM VIEWS THE WORLD and history as a household run by God. In this household-world, God is dispensing or administering affairs according to His own will and in various stages of revelation over the course of time. These various stages mark off distinguishably different economies in the outworking of God's plan for the ages. These economies or administrations are known as dispensations. Understanding these different economies is essential to a proper interpretation of God's revelation within those economies. The dispensations have nothing to do with how people are saved from their sin; instead, they focus on God's purpose for a specific era of history.

With regard to Bible prophecy and chronology, dispensationalism is very important. The dispensational view of literal interpretation supports a futurist perspective that many biblical passages have a yet-future fulfillment. Dispensationalism also maximizes the linear view of history, teaching that history has a beginning and an end. Thus, there is built into the dispensational view a certain chronology of events where it makes sense that certain eras precede other eras or dispensations. It may be true that some elements within the progress of history are cyclical, such as the repetitive deeds of fallen mankind. But history is not cyclical because it has a beginning followed by progressive testing, resulting in a climax of events.

The late Charles Ryrie noted that *The Oxford English Dictionary* defines a theological dispensation as "a stage in a progressive revelation, expressly adopted to the needs of a particular nation or period of time...also, the age or period during which a system has prevailed." The English word *dispensation* translates the Greek noun *oikonomía*, often rendered "administration" in most modern translations. The verb *oikonoméô* refers to a manager of a household. "In the New Testament," noted Ryrie, "*dispensation* means to manage or administer the affairs of a household, as, for example, in the Lord's story of the unfaithful steward in Luke 16:1-13."[1]

The Greek word *oikonomía* is a compound of *oikos*, meaning "house," and *nomos*, meaning "law." Taken together, "the central idea in the word *dispensation* is that of managing or administering the affairs of a household."[2]

Ryrie continued:

> The various forms of the word *dispensation* are used in the New Testament twenty times. The verb *oikonoméô* is used in Luke 16:2 where it is translated "to be a steward." The noun *oikonómos* is used ten times (Luke 12:42; 16:1, 3, 8; Romans 16:23; I Cor. 4:1, 2; Galatians 4:2; Titus 1:7; I Pet. 4:10), and in all instances it is translated "steward" except "chamberlain" in Romans 16:23. The noun *oikonomía* is used nine times (Luke 16:2, 3, 4; I Cor. 9:17; Eph. 1:10; 3:2, 9; Col. 1:25; I Tim. 1:4). In these instances it is translated variously ("stewardship," "dispensation," "edifying"). The Authorized Version of Ephesians 3:9 has "fellowship" (*koinonia*), whereas the American Standard Version has "dispensation."[3]

Dr. Ryrie noted the following characteristics of dispensationalism:

- two parties are always involved
- specific responsibilities
- accountability as well as responsibility
- a change may be made at any time unfaithfulness is found in the existing administration
- God is the one to whom men are responsible
- faithfulness is required of the subordinate party
- a stewardship may end at any time
- dispensations are connected with the mysteries of God
- dispensations and ages are connected ideas
- there are at least three dispensations (likely seven)[4]

The *definition* of a dispensation, according to Ryrie, is "a distinguishable economy in the outworking of God's plan."[5] A *description* of dispensationalism would include the following:

- distinctive revelation
- testing
- failure
- judgment
- a continuance of certain ordinances valid until then
- an annulment of other regulations until then valid
- a fresh introduction of new principles not before valid
- the progressive revelation of God's plan for history[6]

The chart in this chapter focuses upon the chronological sequence of the dispensations and whether or not a dispensation applies only to the era of its jurisdiction or continues beyond. For example, many aspects of human government, promise, and Israel continue past their own time period. On the other hand, innocence, conscience, the church age, and the Millennium are limited to their distinct ages. Technically, the Tribulation period is a continuance of Israel's dispensation because it is the completion of Daniel's seventieth week. It is important to recognize that the Mosaic Law aspect of the dispensation of Israel was fulfilled by Christ at His first coming, while the prophetic aspects continue into the future.

Many people have believed in *dispensations* or *periodization* without adhering to the system of theology known as dispensationalism. Dispensationalism combines a view of the dispensations with what Dr. Ryrie calls the three *sine qua nons* (Latin, "that without which") or *essentials* of dispensationalism.[7] These are not a definition or description of dispensationalism; instead, they are basic theological tests that can be applied to an individual to see whether or not he is a dispensationalist. The three are in the following order:

- *consistent* literal interpretation
- a distinction between God's plan for Israel and His plan for the church
- the goal of history is the glory of God in a multifaceted way

We believe the theology known today as dispensationalism can be said to at least generally represent what the Bible teaches, especially as

The Dispensations

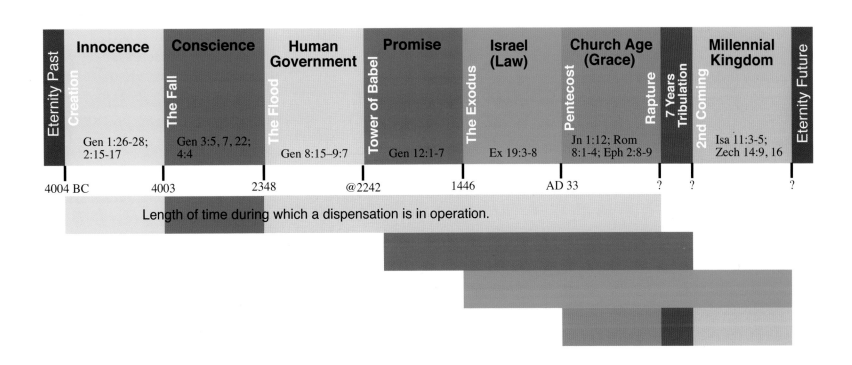

Eternity Past	Innocence	Conscience	Human Government	Promise	Israel (Law)	Church Age (Grace)		Millennial Kingdom	Eternity Future

Creation — Gen 1:26-28; 2:15-17

The Fall — Gen 3:5, 7, 22; 4:4

The Flood — Gen 8:15–9:7

Tower of Babel — Gen 12:1-7

The Exodus — Ex 19:3-8

Pentecost — Jn 1:12; Rom 8:1-4; Eph 2:8-9

Rapture

7 Years Tribulation

2nd Coming — Isa 11:3-5; Zech 14:9, 16

4004 BC   4003   2348   @2242   1446   AD 33   ?   ?   ?

Length of time during which a dispensation is in operation.

it relates to Bible prophecy. And, as far as we know, it is the only view that takes all the chronology of Scripture literally. To view the Bible dispensationally is to view God's plan for history, including its chronology, from His perspective.

What are the dispensations or ages in history? There are seven that can be deduced from God's Word:

- *Innocence* (Genesis 1:28–3:6)—This apparently was the shortest of the dispensations and ended in the fall into sin by Adam and Eve, the parents of the human race.

- *Conscience* (Genesis 3:7–8:14)—The title "conscience" comes from Romans 2:15 and designates the time between the Fall and the Flood, during which time humanity's rule of life was the conscience.

- *Human Government* (Genesis 8:15–11:9)—After the Flood, God said He would not judge men directly until the return of Christ at the second coming. Then a human agency known as civil government was divinely established to mediate and attempt to restrain the evil of men.

- *Promise* (Genesis 11:10–Exodus 18:27)—This period is dominated by the call of Abram and the promise that God made to him and his descendants, both physical and spiritual.

- *Israel/Law* (Exodus 19–John 14:30)—Israel was not and never was saved by keeping the Law. Instead, the Law stipulated how the people were to live. The Law was designed to govern every aspect of their lives. But the Law was temporary until the coming of Christ and the fulfillment of the Law by Him.

- *Church/Grace* (Acts 2:1–Revelation 19:21)—The rule of life for the church is grace. Through the church, God's grace is extended to everyone worldwide through the gospel.

- *Millennial kingdom* (Revelation 20:1-15)—During Messiah's 1000-year reign over the earth from His throne in Jerusalem, the promises God made to Israel as a nation will be fulfilled. The church, who is Christ's bride, will also reign with Him. Because Israel will be in her glory, the Gentiles will also reap great blessings as well (Romans 11:30-32).

Dispensational theology enables us to rightly divide God's Word, which provides a framework for understanding God's plan for history. This is important because when we understand God's purpose for each era of history and its proper chronology, we are able to understand God's will for each dispensation. A believer who has a divine perspective on the past, present, and future is able to know what God expects of him in every area of life. The dispensationalist, for example, does not live in this age of grace as if he were still under the rule of the Mosaic Law. Instead, he understands that he is now under the Law of Christ and awaiting the rapture.

POST-FLOOD GENEALOGY

THE POST-FLOOD GENEALOGY is found primarily in Genesis 11, with some data also in Genesis 10. The Genesis 11 genealogy is one of only two instances—out of 39 biblical genealogies (the other is Genesis 5)—in which numbers are provided that enable one to come up with a chronological timeline that runs from the post-Flood era to the call of Abraham (Genesis 12). As in Genesis 5, the fact that a numerical chronology is supported by the data in the text is a clear indication God wants His readers to be aware of the length of time associated with these people and events. As stated earlier, there is nothing in the biblical text that indicates these passages are not a record of real events happening in real history over the time spans God reveals.

The post-Flood genealogy of Genesis 11 should be handled in the same way as the genealogy of Genesis 5, which yields real chronological information that fits a 360-day year. This means we can add the Genesis 11 data to the Genesis 5 data to determine chronological information up to the life of Abraham. Abraham was born 2008 years after Creation, and 352 years after the Flood. Because the total elapsed time from the Creation to our own day has been a couple of decades more than 6000 years, we can determine that Abraham was called by God about a third of the way through history as it has occurred thus far.

Post-Flood Genealogy

Patriarch	Birth Time Span	Running Total Since Creation
The Flood	0	1656
Arpachshad	2	1658
Shelah	35	1693
Eber	30	1723
Peleg	34	1757

Patriarch	Birth Time Span	Running Total Since Creation
Reu	30	1787
Serug	32	1819
Nahor	30	1849
Terah	29	1878
Abraham	130	2008

The Tower of Babel incident took place about 125 years after the Flood. Genesis 10:25 says, "The name of the one was Peleg, for in his days the earth was divided." The noun *Peleg* means "division," and the verbal form is used in the sentence as well. This passage, at minimum, refers to the confusion of the common language (probably some form of Hebrew) into multiple tongues. However, since the Hebrew word for "earth" is used, some believe it could also refer to a splitting of the continents from a single landmass as a result of a cataclysmic event occurring over a few days. If a supernatural dividing of the single landmass into continents and islands occurred in conjunction with the supernatural confusing of the languages, then this would have resulted in a geographic division of people from one another, which would have further reinforced the confusion of the languages.

Post-Flood Genealogy (Genesis 10–11)

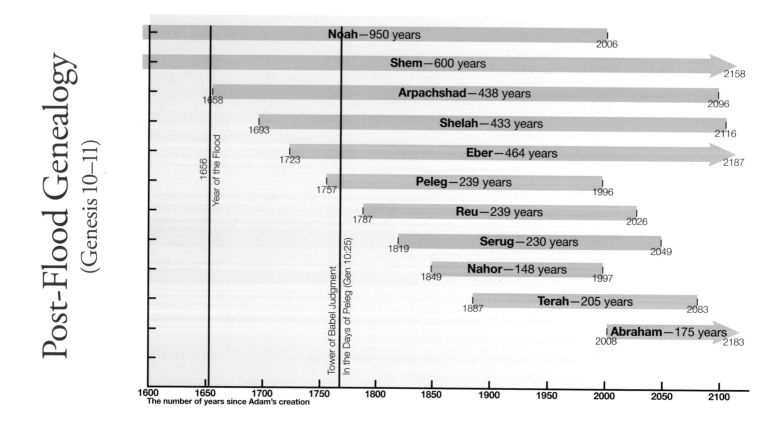

The number of years since Adam's creation

EXPONENTIAL DECAY CURVE

ONE OF THE INDICATORS that the early portion of Genesis is using real data observed from actual history is illustrated in the chart entitled "Exponential Decay Curve." The numbers used in the Genesis 5 and 11 genealogies reflect actual data recorded by Moses in the Hebrew text of the Old Testament and were accurately translated in our English translations. Theologian and scientist Charles Clough compiled the data in Genesis 5 and 11 and plotted a chart that depicts this information from the biblical text. Clough points out "the Bible testifies that…man's whole body was altered. Man's life span began to drop after the flood from an antediluvian average value of 930 years to the value of our present life span of about 70 years."[1] Clough explains his chart as follows:

> [The chart] pictures the values of man's longevity as reported in Gen. 5 and 11. The decline in longevity after the flood presents a vexing riddle to Bible critics. Whereas other accounts of man's longevity in ancient times (such as the Babylonian materials) give disjointed, unrelated high ages, the Genesis account reports a decline that fits the

form of standard exponential "decay curves" (dotted lines in chart). Such curves are usually found when there is a change from one equilibrium state to another in physics, chemistry, and electronics. None of the critics' attempted "explanations" of this decline fit the actual data. Such decay curves cannot be due to calendar changes, guesswork, or sophisticated number games. It must, therefore, be due to a true eye-witness record of a real change of equilibrium state and the resulting decline in man's lifespan.[2]

The fact that there is such a radical change in the average life span of humans from the pre-Flood to the post-Flood worlds indicates that tremendous changes must have taken place. This is confirmed in 2 Peter 3:6, which speaks of the Flood as a "destruction" of the pre-Flood world. Clough says of Peter's commentary on the flood, "In verses 5 and 7, he distinguishes this present world ("the heavens and the earth which are now") from the antediluvian world ("the heavens were of old and the earth…"). By using the vocabulary of Genesis 1:1 ("heavens and earth"), Peter teaches that the flood event marked off two eras of history for not only the planet earth but also the entire heavens!"[3]

A key reason for the Flood was the rampant sinfulness of mankind. "The LORD saw that the wickedness of man was great on the earth, and that every intent of the thoughts of his heart was only evil continually" (Genesis 6:5). However, the Flood did not wash away man's sin nature: "The LORD smelled the soothing aroma; and the LORD said to Himself, 'I will never again curse the ground on account of man, for the intent of man's heart is evil from his youth; and I will never again destroy every living thing, as I have done'" (Genesis 8:21). Because the threat of direct judgment no longer remained for sinful mankind, God shortened the human life span drastically and further cursed the ground so that man would not have as much "idle time" to descend into greater sinfulness. A shorter life span is one of the restraints God imposed after the Flood to keep humanity in check until the final judgment and destruction of the current heavens and earth (2 Peter 3:10-13).

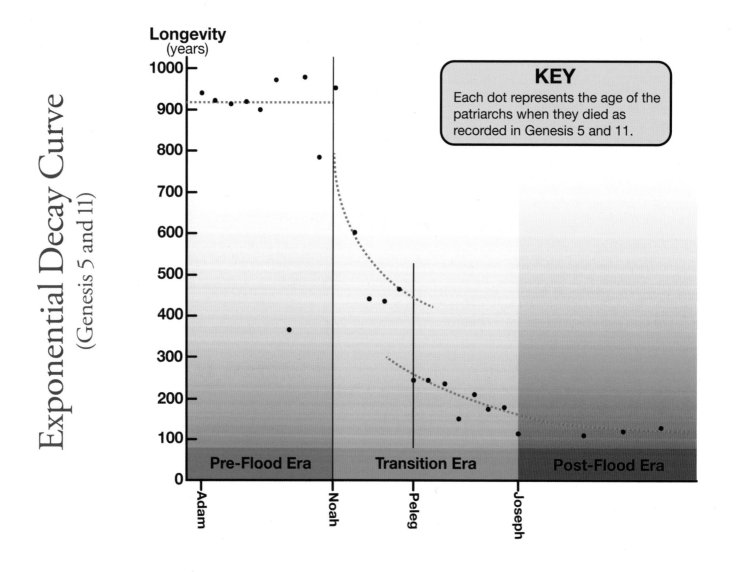

KEY
Each dot represents the age of the patriarchs when they died as recorded in Genesis 5 and 11.

TEN DESCENDANTS IN ONE GENERATION

THE SHIFT FROM THE PRE-FLOOD to the post-Flood world brought about many changes. According to Genesis 8:21, the global Flood was an additional curse over and above the original curse of Genesis 3:13-18. We also learn from Genesis 8:21 that this will be the final curse imposed upon humanity until the Tribulation. God's promise in verse 22 provides stability to creation until God intervenes in history again at Christ's second coming. (The basis for modern science is the assumption that nature is stable and allows for repeatable regularity in the universe. The common belief during the late Middle Ages among Christians provided just such a belief that led to the rise of modern science.) The student of Scripture can observe this transition from the pre-Flood to the post-Flood world in the sudden decline in life spans after the Flood.

We know that four men transitioned from the pre-Flood world to the post-Flood one: Noah, Shem, Ham, and Japheth. Only Noah (Genesis 9:29) and Shem (Genesis 11:11) have their ages recorded in Scripture. The life spans of Ham and Japheth are not recorded, but they likely lived hundreds of years after the Flood, like Shem, who lived 502 of his 600 years after the Flood. Noah lived 350 of his 950 years after the Flood. The fact that Noah, his sons, and their wives had lived in the pre-Flood world enabled the transition to the post-Flood world to develop with a body of knowledge and wisdom from the pre-Flood world. This means that Noah and his family were the founders of the post-Flood world—with them, humanity got a new start. The post-Flood world began with a clear knowledge of God and what He required from mankind. Of particular interest is the fact that Noah died a year after Abraham was born, about 350 years after the Flood. Shem was still alive during most of Abraham's life. Scripture does not tell us if there was direct interaction between Abraham and Shem, but it's possible that could have taken place.

As a result of the decline of life spans after the Flood, there came a unique period of time during which ancestors outlived their descendants, and ten generations of ancestors died out within the span of a single generation. For a few hundred years after the Flood, one could talk with individuals who had lived in the pre-Flood world and find out what it was like. Then within the span of a single generation, those sources of knowledge and wisdom were gone. One possible result of this was that those who rejected God's Word (in a similar fashion as those described in Romans 1:21-23) went on to corrupt the memories of the pre-Flood world by spreading mythological tales about it. Only the Word of God, then, preserves an accurate and trustworthy history of the pre-Flood world.

The post-Flood genealogies reflect the real history of degraded life spans after the "increased curse" was instituted by God following the Flood. People who lived before the Flood had an average life span of 930 years, excluding Enoch, who was taken to heaven without dying. After a 300- to 500-year post-Flood transition, the average life span settled down to around 70 or 80 years, as indicated by Moses in Psalm 90:10. During this transition period, ten generations of individuals died within the time span of a single generation—something that will never again occur in history.

Ten Descendants Die in One Generation
(Genesis 11)

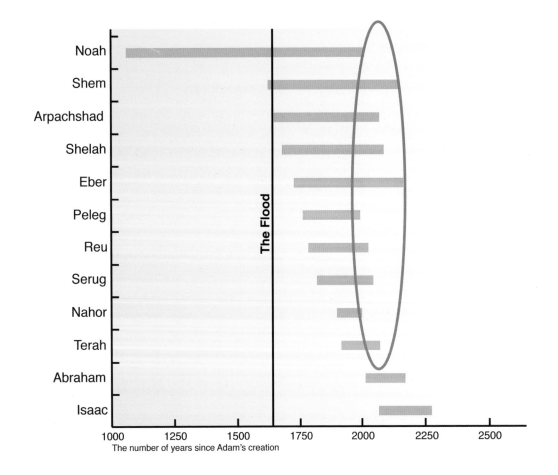

The number of years since Adam's creation

FROM THE FLOOD TO THE CALL OF ABRAHAM

AFTER THE FLOOD there was a sense of new beginnings for humanity. Even though this new start was comprised of a community of eight people who were all believers, Scripture repeats the pre-Flood statement characterizing the antediluvian community: "for the intent of man's heart is evil from his youth" (Genesis 8:21). Not surprisingly, the record of the post-Flood world is that humanity was traveling down the same road of decline as before the Flood. Nimrod, the founder of both Babel and Nineveh, stirred up people in rebellion against God by constructing the Tower of Babel, which represented the corporate rebellion of mankind against God. This act of shaking mankind's fist in the face of God seems to imply that the corporate effort could insulate them against God's judgment. But God came down and confused their single language, which caused these rebels to disperse (Genesis 11:5-9).

This corporate rebellion took place around 2182 BC, about 166 years after the Flood. In the post-Flood genealogy recorded in Genesis 11, we see that God's further cursing of the earth had greatly shortening mankind's life span. The genealogy of Shem is recorded from Arpachshad to Terah (eight generations later), who was the father of Abram. In both the pre-Flood genealogy of Genesis 5 and the post-Flood narrative of chapter 11 we see the same pessimism regarding humanity—people were on the same vector of decline that had taken place before the Flood.

However, the call of Abram in Genesis 12 brings hope into the world. With this call, God has decided to counter the rise of the kingdom of man. He chooses Abram and cuts a covenant with him (Genesis 15:1-21). This marks the humble beginnings of the kingdom of God on earth, which will eventually culminate in the millennial reign of Christ, during which He will rule on earth for 1000 years. God's great movement began very small, with a man who had no children. God changed this man's name from Abram to Abraham, which means "father of many nations." Abraham's promised son, Isaac, was not born until Abraham had reached the age of 100 and his wife, Sarah, had turned 90. This great plan didn't start playing itself out until after the kingdom of man was established by Nimrod. Most of the rest of the Bible is a record of the ups and downs of the outworking of God's plan for the redemption of humanity—a plan that started out small, but will one day rule over both heaven and earth.

The Lord called Abram out of Ur of the Chaldeans and made an unconditional covenant, or contract, with him. This contract, known as the Abrahamic Covenant, contained three major provisions: (1) a land to Abram and his descendants Israel, (2) a seed or physical descendants of Abraham, and (3) a worldwide blessing (Genesis 12:1-3).

In order to make His point clear, the Lord put Abram to sleep and made Himself the only signatory of the contract (Genesis 15:1-21). God told Abram, "To your descendants I have given this land" (verse 18). Even though the Lord was the only active signatory to the cutting of the covenant, it is clear that Abraham obeyed the Lord during his lifetime: "Abraham obeyed Me and kept My charge, My commandments, My statutes and My laws" (Genesis 26:5). This covenant was repeated to Abraham, Isaac, and Jacob and their descendants a little more than 20 times in the book of Genesis alone (Genesis 12:1-3,7-9; 13:14-18; 15:1-18; 17:1-27; 22:15-19; 26:2-6,24-25; 27:28-29,38-40; 28:1-4,10-22; 31:3,11-13; 32:22-32; 35:9-15; 48:3-4,10-20; 49:1-28; 50:23-25). God's promise to the patriarchs is said to be an everlasting covenant (Genesis 17:7,13,19).

Even though things were not looking good generations after the Flood, the Lord brought hope into the world through the Abrahamic Covenant. This covenant was the most important one with regard to God's implementation of His plan for humanity.

The Flood to Abraham
(Genesis 10–12)

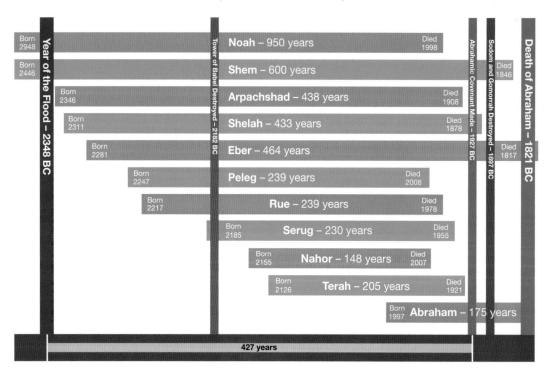

	Born		Died
Noah – 950 years	2948		1998
Shem – 600 years	2446		1846
Arpachshad – 438 years	2346		1908
Shelah – 433 years	2311		1878
Eber – 464 years	2281		1817
Peleg – 239 years	2247		2008
Rue – 239 years	2217		1978
Serug – 230 years	2185		1955
Nahor – 148 years	2155		2007
Terah – 205 years	2126		1921
Abraham – 175 years	1997		

Year of the Flood – 2348 BC
Tower of Babel Destroyed – 2182 BC
Abrahamic Covenant Made – 1927 BC
Sodom and Gomorrah Destroyed – 1897 BC
Death of Abraham – 1821 BC

427 years

THE PATRIARCHS

T HE PATRIARCHS WERE the forefathers of the people of Israel. The book of Genesis focuses specifically on four great patriarchs of the Jewish family: Abraham, Isaac, Jacob, and Joseph. God's redemptive promises were given to Abraham's descendants and ultimately culminated in the messianic line through Jacob's son Judah. While Joseph was not in that line, he played a significant role in helping preserve the family while they were in Egypt.

Abraham

According to the Abrahamic Covenant as stated in Genesis 12:2-7, God would give Abraham's descendants land, seed, and blessing. Through these descendants, the whole world would ultimately be blessed as well. The promises of the Abrahamic Covenant would later be restated throughout the Old Testament: (1) The land promise would be renewed in the Mosaic Covenant (Deuteronomy 29–30); (2) the promised seed would be stated in the Davidic Covenant (2 Samuel 7:16); (3) the blessing promise would be clarified in the prediction of the New Covenant (Jeremiah 31:31-34).

The story of Abraham's faith reached an initial climax when he formally "cut a covenant" with God (Genesis 15:12-17). Instead of joining Abraham in a *conditional* promise made by both parties, God alone divided the animals in half and passed through them, indicating that He alone would keep this promise as an *unconditional* covenant.

When God's promise that Abraham would have a son of "his own body" (15:4) didn't immediately come to fruition, barren Sarah suggested that her servant girl, Hagar, serve as a surrogate mother. Hagar became pregnant and later gave birth to Ishmael ("God hears"), the ancestor of the Arab peoples. God made it clear that Ishmael wasn't the son that had been promised to Abraham and Sarah. Even so, God twice spared Ishmael's life (16:7-15; 21:14-21), promising to make him a "great nation."

Isaac

The miraculous birth of Isaac to Abraham and Sarah both initiated the messianic line and was a foreshadow of the miraculous birth of Jesus, who would culminate the promised line. The birth of

The Patriarchs
(Genesis 12–50)

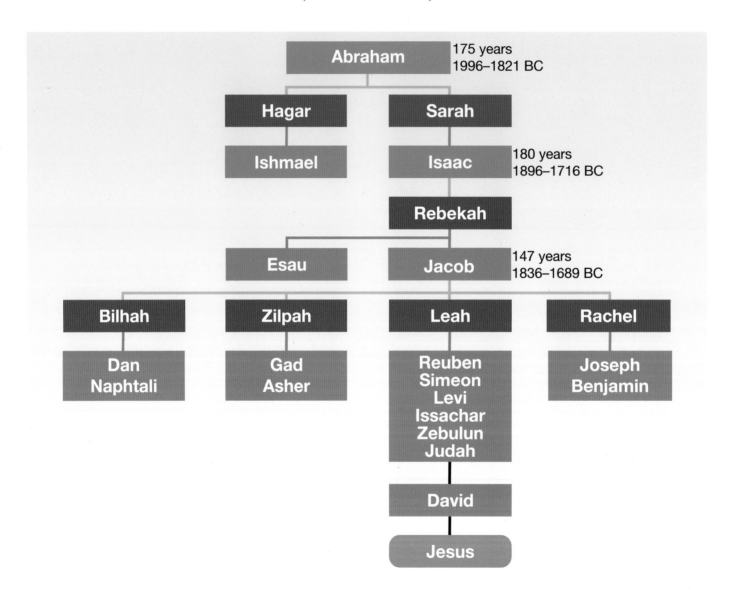

Abraham — 175 years, 1996–1821 BC

Hagar
Sarah

Ishmael
Isaac — 180 years, 1896–1716 BC

Rebekah

Esau
Jacob — 147 years, 1836–1689 BC

Bilhah
Zilpah
Leah
Rachel

Dan
Naphtali

Gad
Asher

Reuben
Simeon
Levi
Issachar
Zebulun
Judah

Joseph
Benjamin

David

Jesus

Isaac (meaning "laughter") caused Sarah to laugh with God, instead of laughing at Him (cf. 18:12-15; 21:6-7). Years later, God tested Abraham's faith and asked him to sacrifice Isaac on Mount Moriah (22:1-16). Abraham passed this test of faith, knowing "God will provide" a lamb, and He did.

Later, Abraham sent one of his servants to Haran to seek a bride for Isaac, and God led the servant to Rebekah (Genesis 24). While God indeed did bless Ishmael (25:12-18), He kept the covenant promises with Isaac (26:1-16). All through the book of Genesis, God continued to narrow the promised line. It would come through Isaac, not Ishmael. In time, Rebekah became pregnant with twin boys, Esau and Jacob (25:21-28). God promised the line would pass through the younger one, Jacob.

Jacob

It was typical in the ancient Middle East for the eldest son to receive both the *birthright* (position of leadership) and the *blessing* (double portion) from the father. However, Esau "despised" the birthright and traded it for a bowl of soup (Genesis 25:27-34). Later, Jacob deceived his father into giving him the blessing. This enraged Esau, and Jacob had to flee to Haran. Despite Jacob's deception, God promised to bring Jacob back to the land and reconfirmed the covenant with him (28:10-17).

While Jacob lived in Haran, he married Leah and Rachel, the daughters of Laban, his mother's brother. From these marriages (and from their handmaids) would come 12 sons who would become the ancestors of the 12 tribes of Israel (Genesis 29:1–30:4). After residing in Haran for 20 years, Jacob returned to Canaan with his family and settled there. En route, he wrestled with an angel of the Lord (Hosea 12:4), who changed his name to Israel.

Joseph

Genesis 37–50 focuses on Joseph, whom God used to relocate the patriarchal family to Egypt. God's selection of this younger brother (one of Rachel's children) follows a pattern that appears throughout Genesis. At first things didn't look good, however. Joseph's ten older brothers were envious of him and sold him to slave traders who took him to Egypt. There, God blessed him and eventually exalted him as the grand vizier of Pharaoh (41:37-46). Years later, the entire family was reconciled, reunited, and moved to Egypt under Joseph's blessing and protection (Genesis 45–46).

While God certainly used Joseph to bless the rest of the family, Jacob promised that the "scepter" of leadership would go to Judah, one of Leah's children (49:10). This messianic promise teaches that the ruler's staff would remain in Judah "until the one comes to whom it belongs" (Hebrew, *Shiloh*).

The book of Genesis closes with the patriarchal family living in Egypt. And while Joseph was on his death bed, he promised the Israelites that God would eventually lead them out of Egypt and back to the Promised Land (50:24-25).

FROM BONDAGE TO THE EXODUS

THE BOOK OF EXODUS tells the story of the Israelites' exit from bondage in Egypt. It is a powerful drama of betrayal, slavery, emancipation, and liberation. Exodus is a narrative account of the history of the descendants of Jacob (Israel) from the death of Joseph in circa 1805 BC (Exodus 1:1-7) to the construction of the tabernacle in the wilderness in 1446 BC (Exodus 40:17). The biblical account includes the years of Israel's bondage and servitude in Egypt, the call of Moses, the confirmation with Pharaoh, the mass exodus of the Israelites from Egypt, and Israel's arrival at Mount Sinai to receive the Law from God Himself.

Hyksos Intermediate Period

During Joseph's lifetime, the ruling dynasty of Pharaohs of the Middle Kingdom Period remained favorable to the Israelites. Even after Joseph's death, the dynasty still showed appreciation for all that Joseph had done for Egypt. However, in time a "new pharaoh" (literally, a new dynasty) arose over Egypt (Exodus 1:8). Conservative Bible scholars associate this transition with the Hyksos invasion, which resulted in a period of Israelite bondage during which the cities of Pithom and Rameses were built (Exodus 1:11). The years of servitude continued for the Israelites even after the Hyksos were expelled in 1570 BC.

New Kingdom Period

The period following the Hyksos intermediate era is known in Egyptian history as the New Kingdom Period, which began with the rule of Ahmose I. Interestingly, several of the rulers of this era had *mose* as part of their name, perhaps indicating the desire of Pharaoh's daughter to see her adopted son Moses become one of those rulers. It is also interesting to note that a famous female ruler named Hatshepsut rose to power over Egypt during the time of Moses. When her father, Thutmose I, died with no surviving male heir old enough to rule, his daughter, Queen Hatshepsut, seized the throne and ruled for more than 20 years without an heir of her own. Many conservative scholars

From Bondage to the Exodus

	1570-1546	Ahmose I	Hyksos expelled
	1546-1526	Amenhotep I	Eighteenth dynasty secured
	1526-1518	Thutmose I	Moses born in Egypt
	1518-1804	Thutmose II	Moses in Pharaoh's court
	1504-1482	Hatshepsut	"She king" of Egypt
	1504-1450	Thutmose III	Pharaoh of oppression
	1453-1415	Amenhotep II	Pharaoh of Exodus
	1415-1401	Thutmose IV	Israel in the Wilderness
	1401-1364	Amenhotep III	Joshua's conquest of Canaan

Timeline markers: 1570 BC, 1540, 1510, 1480, 1450, 1420, 1390, 1360

Wilderness

Date	Reference	Event
day 15, month 1, year 1 1446 BC	Ex 12	The exodus
day 15, month 2, year 1	Ex 16:1	Arrival in Wilderness of Zin
month 3, year 1	Ex 19:1	Arrival in Wilderness of Sinai
day 15, month 1, year 1 1445 BC	Ex 40:1,17 Nu 7:1 Nu 8:1-26	Erection of Tabernacle Dedication of altar Consecration of Levites
day 14, month 1, year 2	Nu 9:5	Passover
day 1, month 2, year 2	Nu 1:2, 18	Census
day 14, month 2, year 2	Nu 9:11	Supplemental Passover
day 20, month 2, year 2	Nu 10:11	Departure from Sinai
month 1, year 40 1406 BC	Nu 20:1	In Wilderness of Zin
day 1, month 5, year 40	Nu 20: 22-29; 33:38	Death of Aaron
day 1, month 11, year 40	Dt 1:3	Moses' address

Based on John MacArthur, *The MacArthur Bible Handbook*
(Nashville, TN: Thomas Nelson, 2003), p. 20.

have speculated that she could well have been "pharaoh's daughter" who found baby Moses in the basket in the Nile River (Exodus 2:5-10). She was forced to marry her half-brother by a lesser wife, who ruled as Thutmose II, but when he died, she ruled alone, suppressing the rise of Thutmose III, who was too young to rule.

Hatshepsut was eventually succeeded by Thutmose III, whom many identify as the Pharaoh who oppressed the Hebrew slaves. He would have been on the throne during the years of Moses' exile in the Sinai wilderness. Next, his son Amenhotep II took the throne and ruled for 26 years. Accepting the 1446 BC date for the exodus would mean that Amenhotep II was most likely the Pharaoh of the exodus.[1] The succession of the rulers of this era can be seen in the chart on page 57.

In Exodus 7–12, we find a detailed account of the ten plagues God sent upon Egypt in response to Pharaoh's refusal to let the Hebrew people leave Egypt. After the tenth and final plague, which resulted in the death of the firstborn Egyptians, the Hebrews (Israelites) left Egypt in a massive exodus into the Sinai wilderness. After celebrating the first Passover in Egypt, the Israelites miraculously crossed the parted Red Sea and eventually made their way to Mount Sinai. There, Moses received the Ten Commandments and God's laws for governing the civil, social, and spiritual life of Israel's people. The covenant was confirmed with the Lord (Yahweh or Jehovah), and then the tabernacle of worship, as well as the Ark of the Covenant, were constructed. The Levitical priesthood was established along with a prescribed system of sacrificial offerings.

During the second year of the wilderness journey a census was taken of all the men age 20 and older (Numbers 1:1-2). These 603,550 men were designated as being old enough to serve in Israel's army (Numbers 1:45-46). This indicates that the total number of people, including women and children, would have been between two to three million. Eventually Moses selected 12 men (one from each tribe) to spy out the land of Canaan (Numbers 13:1-15). When all but two (Joshua and Caleb) returned with a negative report, the people wept aloud and turned back in unbelief against God at Kadesh Barnea.

16

THE FIVE CYCLES OF COVENANTAL CURSING

THERE WERE TWO OCCASIONS on which the Lord made a covenant with Israel after their exodus from Egypt. The first covenant and giving of the Law is found in Exodus 19–24. While Moses was up on the mountain receiving the Law, the nation immediately slipped into idolatry and the covenant was broken. The second cutting of the covenant and giving of God's Law is found in the entire book of Deuteronomy. In both Exodus and Deuteronomy there are "blessing and cursing" sections that explain to the people the blessings that would result when they obeyed God and the curses that would come if they did not obey the Lord (Exodus 23; Deuteronomy 28).

Also, Leviticus 26 evidences a striking similarity with Deuteronomy 28, except that Leviticus 26 presents the curses (Leviticus 26:14-39) within the framework of five progressive stages. Each stage was to increase by a factor of seven (Leviticus 26:18,21,24,28), and at the fifth stage, there would be devastation and deportation from the land. However, the chapter ends with hope that if they repented of their sin while in exile, they would be brought back to the land and

receive blessing (Leviticus 26:40-46). There are many significant parallels between the blessings and curses that appear in Leviticus 26 and Deuteronomy 28.

Deuteronomy 28 provides the most expansive account of the blessing and cursing section of the Mosaic Law. After having enumerated the relatively short list of blessings that God would bestow upon Israel in the land (Deuteronomy 28:1-14), Moses declared the much longer list of curses that God would inflict upon His people when they disobeyed Him (Deuteronomy 28:15-68). The Lord would start by inflicting mild curses at the inception of disobedience, and gradually turn up the heat as insubordination persisted (Leviticus 26:14-17). The most severe chastisement the Lord would inflict upon His wayward people was expulsion, which would occur through the agency of a foreign invader (Deuteronomy 28:49-68). The Lord's logic was something along the line that if Israel did not want to obediently serve Him in their own land, then they could go and serve other gods outside the land (Deuteronomy 28:47-48).

The chart in this chapter focuses upon the cyclical nature of

Five Cycles of Covenantal Cursing
(Leviticus 26)

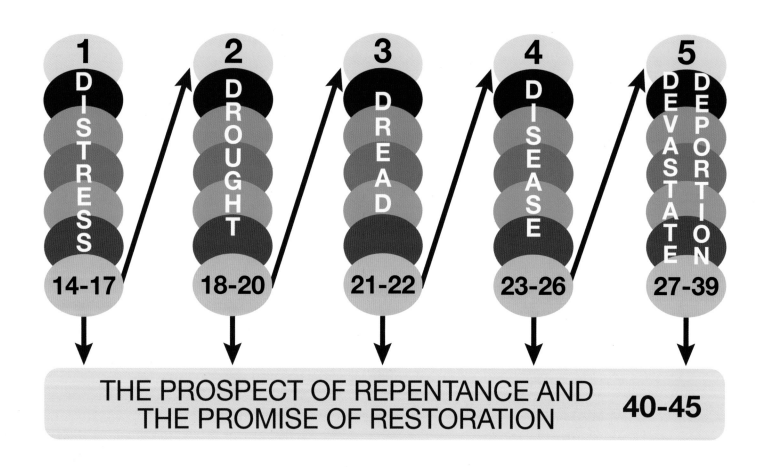

THE PROSPECT OF REPENTANCE AND
THE PROMISE OF RESTORATION **40-45**

Leviticus 26. Scholars have long recognized the cyclical nature of the book of Joshua, and it is possible that the events described in Joshua are the working out of the cycles of discipline stated in Leviticus 26. While Leviticus 26 features cycles, they are not an endless series of cycles; instead, they are progressive in nature and they move toward a goal.

The *first cycle* (Leviticus 26:14-17) was marked by psychological distress, which led to a decline in the health of the nation and loss of agricultural prosperity. The people would suffer from fear, terror, and death in combat. This cycle started out small and was repeated seven times, each cycle stronger than the previous one.

The *second cycle* (Leviticus 26:18-20) was that of drought upon the land of Israel—a serious consequence because ancient Israel depended heavily on its agriculture-based economy. This drought would be experienced in seven phases of recession and lead ultimately to a full depression. Over the course of the seven phases, things would go from bad to worse.

The *third cycle* (Leviticus 26:21-22) would lead to psychological dread as a result of wild animals ravaging the people. These wild animals would kill some of their children and livestock and stir such great fear that most people refuse to venture out. Again, the cycle would start out small and increase sevenfold.

The *fourth cycle* (Leviticus 26:23-26) was marked by disease and pestilence that resulted in death. As with the other cycles of discipline, it started off slow and increased seven times in intensity. As a result, the nation would become weak and vulnerable to their enemies. It would also be a time of increasing hunger and starvation.

In the *fifth cycle* (Leviticus 26:27-39), God would bring devastation upon the nation and the people would be deported to a foreign land. This too would occur in a sevenfold process. This judgment became reality for the Northern Kingdom in 721 BC, when the Assyrians invaded the kingdom and took the people into captivity. The Southern Kingdom was destroyed and taken into captivity in 586 BC by the Babylonians. In AD 70 the entire nation was sent into worldwide captivity by the Romans, and again in AD 135.

Leviticus 26:40-45 promises the people of Israel that at any point in this process, they can repent and access the grace of God and be restored to their land and live in prosperity. Indeed, this will occur during the future time known as the Tribulation, when the Jewish people will come to believe that Jesus is their Messiah, and they will dwell in the land of Israel for 1000 years during Jesus' millennial reign on earth.

THE NATION OF ISRAEL

THE NATION OF ISRAEL began with God's promise to Abraham more than 4000 years ago. God called him to leave his ancient homeland in Ur of the Chaldees to go to a land that He promised to give to Abraham's descendants. There, the Lord told him, "I will make you into a great nation" (Genesis 12:2). In the pages of Scripture that follow, we begin to trace the roots of that nation in the patriarchal families of Abraham, Isaac, and Jacob. Eventually we see the entire family of Jacob (also called *Israel*) move to Egypt, where they are later put into bondage by the Egyptians.

The Exodus

The next great chapter in Israel's history includes their miraculous and dramatic exodus from Egypt under Moses, and their arrival at Mount Sinai so they could receive God's laws and commandments. These become the basis of Israelite society. The provisions of the Mosaic Covenant (Exodus 19–40) explained the theocratic nation's organization and social structure under God's sovereign kingship. As such, the Israelites were to be a holy nation and a kingdom of God on earth. Thus, the Mosaic Covenant offered the nation the opportunity to be the vessel by which God would communicate His redemptive purposes to the rest of mankind.

The Conquest

In order to fulfill His land promise, God led the Israelites, through Joshua, to conquer the land of Canaan, which He had earlier promised to Abraham's descendants (Genesis 15:18-21). The conquest resulted in the 12 tribes of Israel settling in the Promised Land. There, the nation took root in the soil in fulfillment of God's promises. While the land was given to them unconditionally (Genesis 15:16-18), the promise of God's continued blessing upon them depended on their obedience to Him (Deuteronomy 6:10-19; 8:1-20; 28:1-26). The people's failure to maintain all they conquered led to the chaotic era of the judges and the people's desire for a king "like all the nations" (1 Samuel 8:4-5). God gave them what they wanted and appointed King Saul, who was ultimately defeated by the Philistines and died on a battlefield (1 Samuel 31:1-13).

The Davidic Kingdom

Upon Saul's death, David became the king of Judah and ruled at Hebron. Later, he conquered Jerusalem and made it the capital of all Israel (2 Samuel 5:3-10). The apex of Israel's kingdom was reached during the reigns of David and Solomon. After Solomon's death, the kingdom split into two: Judah became the Southern Kingdom, with Jerusalem as its capital. And Israel became the Northern Kingdom, with Samaria as its capital. In 722 BC, Samaria fell to the Assyrians, and in 586 BC, Jerusalem fell to the Babylonians. God promised the Babylonian captives that He would restore them to their land after 70 years of captivity (Jeremiah 25:11-18).

The Return

In fulfillment of His promise, God raised up Cyrus the Persian to defeat the Babylonians and set the Jews free to return to their own land. Nearly 50,000 returned to rebuild the temple, resettle the land, and reignite the messianic hope. However, as the Old Testament era closed, the long-awaited Deliverer had not yet come (Malachi 4:1-8).

The Intertestamental Period

The 400 years between the end of the Old Testament and the beginning of the New are often called the "silent years" because there was no new prophetic word from God. During these years the Persians were eventually replaced by the Greeks as Alexander the Great conquered the world and Hellenized the Middle East (that is, spread Greek culture). During this time, Antiochus IV Epiphanes severely persecuted the Jews and desecrated the temple. This led to the Maccabean Revolt, led by Jewish zealots who overthrew their Greek overlords and entered into a time of relative independence under the Hasmoneans.

The New Testament Era

In time, the Romans replaced the Greeks as the dominant world power. The New Testament opens with Augustus Caesar and the Romans ruling over Israel, which they had divided into subsections: Judea, Samaria, Galilee, Perea, and the Decapolis. During this time, various religious parties strove for leadership among the Jewish people: Sadducees, Pharisees, Herodians, and Essenes. It was into this era that Jesus was born, ministered, died, and rose from the dead. The Gospels and Acts record the specific names of various Roman authorities during that time, which makes it possible to create an accurate chronology of Jesus' life and the time of the early apostles.

The Diaspora

The Jewish revolt against the Romans (AD 66–70) eventually resulted in the destruction of the Second Temple and the city of Jerusalem. A second Jewish revolt in AD 132–135, led by Bar Kochba, also had devastating results on the Jewish people. Between the two revolts, more than one million Jews were killed, resulting in a significant expulsion from their ancient homeland, leaving only a remnant. From then until the twentieth century, the vast majority of the Jewish population was scattered throughout Europe, Asia, and Africa, yet maintained the hope that one day they would be able to return to their beloved homeland.

The Diaspora years have generally been divided into five periods:

1. *Roman and Byzantine Era* (135–638). Under the direction of the Roman emperor Hadrian, Jerusalem was rebuilt as a pagan city and renamed Aelia Capitolina. A pagan temple was constructed on the Temple Mount and the province of Judah was renamed *Palestina* in a deliberate attempt to remove all Jewish identity from the region. Later, when Emperor Constantine converted to Christianity, he moved his capital to Byzantium (renamed Constantinople), and the Christian or Byzantine period extended from 325–638. During this time, the pagan temple on the Temple Mount was removed.

2. *Muslim Domination* (638–1099). Muslim armies took Jerusalem from the Romans in 638. During the seventh century, the Mosque of Omar (Dome of the Rock) and the al-Aqsa Mosque were built on the Temple Mount,

Timeline of National Israel

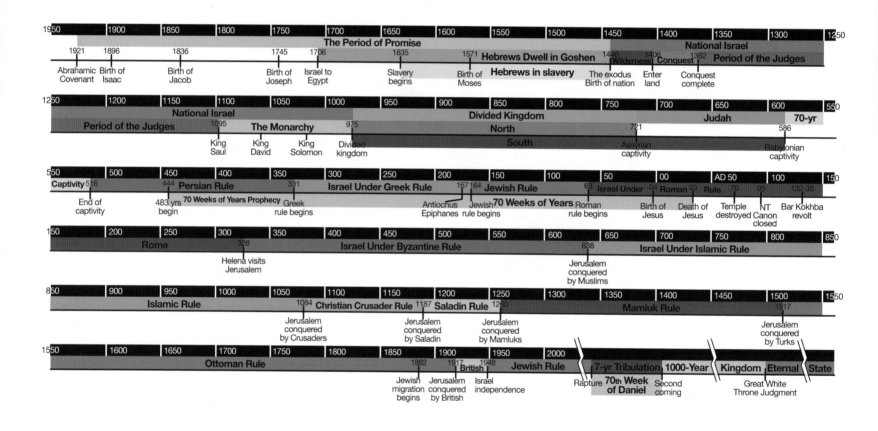

Row 1 (1950–1250 BC):
1950 | 1900 | 1850 | 1800 | 1750 | 1700 | 1650 | 1600 | 1550 | 1500 | 1450 | 1400 | 1350 | 1300 | 1250

The Period of Promise — National Israel

1921 Abrahamic Covenant · 1896 Birth of Isaac · 1836 Birth of Jacob · 1745 Birth of Joseph · 1706 Israel to Egypt · 1635 Slavery begins · 1571 Birth of Moses · Hebrews Dwell in Goshen · Hebrews in slavery · 1446 The exodus / Birth of nation · Wilderness · 1406 Enter land · Conquest · 1362 Conquest complete · Period of the Judges

Row 2 (1250–550 BC):
1250 | 1200 | 1150 | 1100 | 1050 | 1000 | 950 | 900 | 850 | 800 | 750 | 700 | 650 | 600 | 550

National Israel — Divided Kingdom — Judah — 70-yr

Period of the Judges · 1095 · The Monarchy · 975 · North / South · Divided Kingdom

King Saul · King David · King Solomon · Divided kingdom · 721 Assyrian captivity · 586 Babylonian captivity

Row 3 (550 BC–150 AD):
550 | 500 | 450 | 400 | 350 | 300 | 250 | 200 | 150 | 100 | 50 | 00 | AD 50 | 100 | 150

Captivity 516 · 444 Persian Rule · 70 Weeks of Years Prophecy · 331 · Israel Under Greek Rule · 167 · 164 Jewish Rule · 63 Israel Under · 04 Roman 33 Rule · 70 · 95 · 132-35

End of captivity · 483 yrs begin · Greek rule begins · Antiochus Epiphanes · Jewish rule begins · 70 Weeks of Years · Roman rule begins · Birth of Jesus · Death of Jesus · Temple destroyed · NT Canon closed · Bar Kokhba revolt

Row 4 (150–850 AD):
150 | 200 | 250 | 300 | 350 | 400 | 450 | 500 | 550 | 600 | 650 | 700 | 750 | 800 | 850

Rome — Israel Under Byzantine Rule — Israel Under Islamic Rule

326 Helena visits Jerusalem · 638 Jerusalem conquered by Muslims

Row 5 (850–1550 AD):
850 | 900 | 950 | 1000 | 1050 | 1100 | 1150 | 1200 | 1250 | 1300 | 1350 | 1400 | 1450 | 1500 | 1550

Islamic Rule · 1084 Christian Crusader Rule · 1187 Saladin Rule · 1260 · Mamluk Rule · 1517

Jerusalem conquered by Crusaders · Jerusalem conquered by Saladin · Jerusalem conquered by Mamluks · Jerusalem conquered by Turks

Row 6 (1550 AD–):
1550 | 1600 | 1650 | 1700 | 1750 | 1800 | 1850 | 1900 | 1950 | 2000

Ottoman Rule · 1882 · 1917 British · 1948 Jewish Rule · 7-yr Tribulation · 1000-Year Kingdom · Eternal State

Jewish migration begins · Jerusalem conquered by British · Israel independence · Rapture · 70th Week of Daniel · Second coming · Great White Throne Judgment

where they have now stood for nearly 1300 years as symbols of Muslim domination and influence. To this day, their presence has prevented the Jews from rebuilding their own temple on this holy site.

3. *Crusader Period* (1099–1291). Over the course of nearly a century, Jerusalem was conquered by European Catholic warriors in attempts to take back the Holy Land from the Muslims who had desecrated several Christian sites, including the tomb of the Holy Sepulcher. During this time, both Muslims and Jews were slaughtered by the overzealous crusaders, who established the Latin Kingdom of Jerusalem under the auspices of the Roman Catholic Church.

4. *Saladin and Mamluk Periods* (1187–1517). In a renewed call for *jihad* (holy war), Saladin defeated the crusaders at the Horns of Hittim in Galilee on June 30, 1187. By October he took Jerusalem, restoring Muslim control of the city. In 1219, Saladin's nephew ordered the depopulation of the city and destruction of the city's walls in order to keep it from the crusaders. By 1260, the city came under the control of the Mamluks from central Asia, and by 1291, the crusaders were finally driven out of the Holy Land.

5. *Ottoman Turkish Period* (1517–1917). In 1517, Suleiman the Magnificent conquered Jerusalem, taking it from the Mamluks and rebuilding it as a Turkish Muslim city. In 1566, the city walls, which still stand today in the Old City, were completed and Muslim control was maintained. During this era, Jews were forbidden to pray at the Western Wall (Kotel) of the Temple Mount. However, in the nineteenth century, Turkey began to open contact with the West and even permitted some Christians and Jews to settle in Jerusalem.

Modern Era

With the outbreak of World War I (1914–1918), everything changed dramatically in Israel (still called Palestine at that time). The Turks made the fatal mistake of siding with Germany and Kaiser Wilhelm. After Germany and Turkey lost the war, the Allied powers took over Turkey's holdings in the Middle East and Palestine was placed under British rule (1917–1947). During this era, Jewish immigration to the land increased. When the British withdrew in 1948, there were more than 600,000 Jews living in the Promised Land. On May 14, 1948, the Declaration of the Establishment of the State of Israel was proclaimed.

The modern history of Israel has been one of constant struggle and miraculous interventions. Against all odds, Israel won the War of Independence when she was attacked by the combined armies of Egypt, Syria, Saudi Arabia, Lebanon, and Iraq. In 1967, Israel won a stunning military victory over Egypt, Syria, and Jordan in the Six-Day War, recapturing the city of Jerusalem for the first time since the Roman era. In 1973, Israel again was victorious in the three-week-long Yom Kippur War, taking possession of the Golan Heights. In 1991, during the first Gulf War, Iraq launched 42 SCUD missiles at Israel during the time the US-led coalition drove Iraq out of occupied Kuwait. In 2014, Palestinian militants in Gaza fired more than 4500 rockets at Israel. In response, Israel launched Operation Protective Edge with targeted air strikes that destroyed dozens of Palestinian "invasion tunnels" that had been dug underground at the Israeli border.

While Israel's future may seem vulnerable from a human perspective, Scripture proclaims that Israel's future is securely in the hands of God. He has predicted her return, regathering, and future regeneration (Ezekiel 36–39). Every day that passes brings us closer to the final events prophesied in the Word of God.

THE FEASTS OF ISRAEL IN BIBLE PROPHECY

IN LEVITICUS 23, GOD gave to Israel, as a part of the Mosaic Law, seven feasts the people were to celebrate. Each feast was to be celebrated annually, and each one had a special purpose. While most of the feasts were connected with past historical events, all of them served as reminders of certain spiritual truths. For example, Passover was to remind the people that sin cannot be atoned for without the shedding of blood, the Feast of First Fruits was to remind them to put God first in their lives, and the Feast of Tabernacles was a reminder of God's faithfulness.

It seems evident that these seven annual feasts observed by Israel have not only a ceremonial significance, but a prophetic significance as well. With regard to the prophetic aspect, the question is this: Are they fulfilled in relation to Israel, or to the church, or to both? We believe the evidence supports the notion that the prophetic aspect of these feasts is also fulfilled in history in relation to Israel alone. Because there is a prophetic/fulfillment element in the feasts, there is a chronological sequence in history as well.

The seven annual feasts are as follows:

Spring

- Passover (Leviticus 23:5)
- Unleavened Bread (Leviticus 23:6)
- First Fruits (Leviticus 23:10-11)
- Weeks or Pentecost (Leviticus 23:15-17)

Fall

- Trumpets (Leviticus 23:24)
- Day of Atonement (Leviticus 23:27)
- Tabernacles (Leviticus 23:39-43)

It is widely recognized that there is a prophetic aspect to Israel's feast cycle. Christ fulfilled the four feasts in the spring cycle at the exact times they were celebrated on Israel's annual calendar. It appears certain, then, that events related to His second coming will fulfill the three fall feasts. What's more, they will be fulfilled in relation to God's plan for Israel and not God's plan for the church, for the feasts, like the rest of the Mosaic Law, relate to Israel alone. While it's true the fulfillment of Israel's feasts relates to salvation for *all* mankind, the precise prophetic significance and fulfillment relate exclusively to national Israel.

God gave the seven feasts to the Hebrew people to serve as yearly reminders of His promises in the Abrahamic Covenant—promises that He said He would fulfill. These feasts can be fulfilled by and to Israel alone. Thus, the typology of the feasts relate to the Jewish nation only.[1]

This does not mean that the church is not built upon the sacrificial work of Christ on the cross. That is the basis for forgiveness of sin in any dispensation. However, it does mean that the seven feasts do serve as a specific typological prophecy picturing God's plan of redemption for His people Israel.

If we are going to apply the literal method of interpretation consistently, then we cannot see *any* of Israel's feasts being fulfilled by God's program for the church. Why? Because these feasts were given in Leviticus 23 to Israel as part of her law. By contrast, the church has been given the Lord's Table as the feast it is to celebrate *"from now on until* the kingdom of God comes"* (Luke 22:18, emphasis added). If we view any of Israel's feasts as being fulfilled by the church, then we are practicing the same kind of replacement theology that is espoused by those who see the church as completely replacing Israel in God's plan. But nowhere in the New Testament do we see evidence of the church fulfilling any of Israel's feasts. For example, because Israel's feasts are fulfilled only by Israel and not the church, Rosh Hashanah, or the Feast of Trumpets, *cannot* be a foreshadowing of the rapture of the church. Israel's fifth feast does not give any insight into the day of the year on which the rapture will occur.

Dr. Hulbert's summary of the purpose for the fulfillment of Israel's feast makes the best sense within the framework of a *consistent* literal hermeneutic:

> When God fulfilled the first four feasts He had provided everything necessary for Israel to enter into literal kingdom blessing—redemption, separation, resurrection, and the presence of the Holy Spirit. Israel's rejection of these, however, made necessary a national change of heart before the Kingdom could be established. Foreknowing this, God included the Feasts of Trumpets and Day of Atonement in the annual cycle. Thus, the Feast of Trumpets predicted God's alerting of the nation for the impending event which would bring about repentance. The Feast of the Day of Atonement predicted not the death of Christ, which had already been typified in the Passover, but the new reaction of Israel to the Redeemer's death. This change will take place when the believing Remnant repents during the Tribulation period. The event which fulfills this sixth feast is identified as God's intervention to save Israel from destruction as Gentile armies attack Jerusalem.[2]

Dr. Hulbert goes on to say this:

> Israel as a nation officially rejected in turn each spiritual provision offered by God and made available through the fulfillment of the first four feasts. The paschal lamb of God pointed out by John the Baptist was rejected as an imposter. The resurrection of Christ, as it answered to the Feast of Firstfruits, was suppressed in its proclamation by the bribe money paid to the sentries…Finally, the coming of the Spirit was rejected at Pentecost as the Jews taunted the apostles with charges of drunkenness.
>
> By the time of the close of Acts chapter 2, God had done all He could do for Israel until they repented as a nation. Thus, the significance of Peter's second sermon in Acts 3 was that it reemphasized the condition of millennial blessing already laid down in the Old Testament, but as yet unfulfilled…
>
> Of the utmost importance here is the fact that with the shedding of the blood of Christ to take away sin, and with the coming of the Spirit to empower the life of the redeemed, all of the

spiritual requirements for the millennial kingdom had been met as far as God was concerned. But God's provision could not be operative until man appropriated it. This point cannot be over-emphasized, for it is not only the reason for the delay in the fulfillment of the final three feasts, it is the basis for understanding the relationship of the church to the feasts.[3]

The three fall feasts await fulfillment in events that will take place at the second coming of Christ to earth and the Millennium, and their chronology is clear. The Feast of Trumpets will take place at the second coming, as Matthew 24:31 describes: "He will send forth His angels with a great trumpet and they will gather together His elect from the four winds, from one end of the sky to the other." The Day of Atonement will be applied to the nation of Israel when the people realize that Jesus was their long-awaited Messiah all along (Zechariah 12:10; Romans 11:25-27). And the Feast of Tabernacles will be fulfilled by the arrival of the millennial kingdom, when the Jewish nation will dwell with their God in the land of Israel for 1000 years.

Israel's Feasts in History and Prophecy

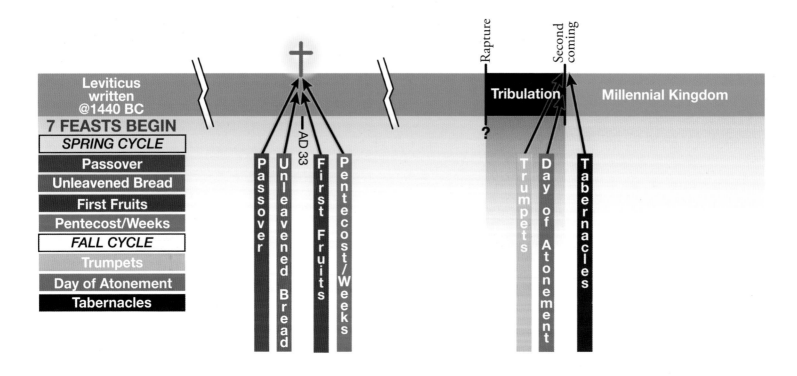

ISRAEL'S PROPHETIC OUTLINE
IN DEUTERONOMY 4

A S THE NATION OF ISRAEL sat perched on the banks of the Jordan River, before she ever set one foot upon the Promised Land, the Lord gave an outline of her entire history through His mouthpiece Moses. Deuteronomy is this revelation, and it is like a road map for where Israel's history was headed before the trip got underway. While different segments of the historical journey have been updated with more details being added along the way, not a single adjustment from the earlier course has ever been made. Part of that journey includes the still-future Tribulation period.

Before we look at God's prophetic road map, it is important that we understand the purpose for the book of Deuteronomy. George Harton provides this overview:

> The purpose of Deuteronomy is to call for new commitment to the covenants by new generations in Israel…The point of the book is not primarily legal (to recite a corpus of law), nor historical (to recount a series of events), but it is hortatory (to preach so as to move Israel to faith and obedience).[1]

As Moses exhorted the nation of Israel, he provided in Deuteronomy 4:25-31 an outline of what would happen to this elect people once they crossed over the Jordan River and settled the land:

> When you become the father of children and children's children and *have remained long in the land, and act corruptly*, and make an idol in the form of anything, and do that which is evil in the sight of the LORD your God so as to provoke Him to anger, I call heaven and earth to witness against you today, that *you will surely perish quickly from the land* where you are going over the Jordan to possess it. You shall not live long on it, but will be utterly destroyed. *The LORD will scatter you among the peoples*, and you will be left few in number among the nations where the LORD drives you. There you will serve gods, the work of man's hands, wood and stone, which neither see nor hear nor eat nor smell. *But from there you will seek the LORD your God*, and you will find Him if you search for Him with all your heart and all your soul. *When you are in*

Israel's Prophetic Outline in Deuteronomy
(Deuteronomy 4)

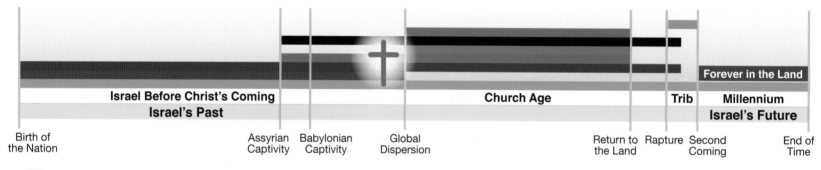

Israel Before Christ's Coming		Church Age	Trib	Millennium
Israel's Past				Israel's Future

Forever in the Land

Birth of the Nation — Assyrian Captivity — Babylonian Captivity — Global Dispersion — Return to the Land — Rapture — Second Coming — End of Time

1) Israel and her descendants would remain long in the land.

2) Israel would act corruptly and slip into idolatry.

3) Israel would be removed from the land.

4) The Lord would scatter her among the nations.

5) Israel would be given over to idolatry during her wanderings among the nations.

6) While dispersed among the nations, Israel would seek and find the Lord when she searched for Him with all her heart.

7) There would come a time of *tribulation*, said to occur in the *latter days*, during which time she would turn to the Lord.

8) "For the LORD your God is a compassionate God; He will not fail you nor destroy you nor forget the covenant with your fathers which He swore to them" (Deut 4:31).

distress and all these things have come upon you, in the latter days you will return to the LORD your God and listen to His voice. For the LORD your God is a compassionate God; He will not fail you nor destroy you nor forget the covenant with your fathers which He swore to them.

In the passage above, we have highlighted in italic type those events that are key elements in the history of Israel. A summary of these events is as follows:

1. Israel and her descendants would remain long in the land.

2. Israel would act corruptly and slip into idolatry.

3. Israel would be removed from the land.

4. The Lord would scatter the people among the nations.

5. Israel would be given over to idolatry during their times of wandering.

6. While dispersed among the nations, Israel would seek and find the Lord when they searched for Him with all their heart.

7. There would come a time of *tribulation,* said to occur in the latter days, during which time they would turn to the Lord.

8. "The LORD your God is a compassionate God; He will not fail you nor destroy you nor forget the covenant with your fathers which He swore to them" (Deuteronomy 4:31).

If the first five events have happened to Israel—and no one would deny that they have—then it is clear from the text that the final events will also occur to the same people in the same way. This is clearest from the context. The Bible does not "change horses in midstream" so that suddenly Israel, the recipient of these curses, is dropped out of the picture and the church takes over and receives the blessings. While there are various systems of theology that espouse such a view, the Bible nowhere teaches this. Any reading of Deuteronomy 4 requires readers to admit that the same recipient is in mind throughout the whole of the text under examination. If that is true, then the last three events have yet to be fulfilled for Israel in the same historical manner in which the first five events took place. Thus, the fulfillment of the final three events is still future. Israel was not rescued as a result of tribulation in AD 70; instead, she was judged. Deuteronomy 4 pictures Israel's return to the Lord after tribulation, not judgment.

In Deuteronomy 4, Moses, under the inspiration of the Holy Spirit, received a prophetic outline for what lay ahead for the newly formed nation of Israel. The events that have already taken place have unfolded in the same order as stated in this prophetic passage. In fact, Moses later expanded upon these prophetic events in Deuteronomy 26–32.

CONQUEST AND CHAOS

THE BOOKS OF JOSHUA AND JUDGES introduce us to periods of incredible victories and disastrous defeats. We follow Joshua and the Israelites as they conquer the Promised Land, only to see their descendants plunge into spiritual compromise, moral confusion, and civil catastrophe. There is no greater contrast in all the Bible between two books that appear in chronological sequence. The remarkably swift conquest was followed by long years of agonizing confusion and chaos.

If we date the exodus at 1446 BC and allow 40 years for the wilderness journey, we arrive at a date of circa 1405 BC for the beginning of the conquest (cf. Exodus 16:35; Numbers 14:34-35). Caleb indicated that he was 40 years old at the time Israel turned back at Kadesh Barnea and 85 at the end of the conquest (Joshua 14:7-10). Thus, 45 years elapsed from the Kadesh Barnea incident to the completion of the conquest. Because Israel wandered in the wilderness for about 38 years after what took place at Kadesh Barnea, the conquest must have taken about 7 years (1406–1399 BC). The conquest is covered in Joshua chapters 1–14, whereas chapters 15–24 document subsequent events that took place between 1399–1374 BC.[1]

The book of Joshua recounts three specific campaigns in which the Israelites acquired the majority of the land from the Canaanites:

Central Campaign (Joshua 6–9)
    Key Cities: Jericho, Ai, Gibeon
Southern Campaign (Joshua 10)
    Key Cities: Jerusalem, Hebron, Lachish
Northern Campaign (Joshua 11)
    Key City: Hazor

Joshua 12:9-24 lists 31 royal city-states conquered by the Israelites under Joshua's leadership. Joshua then allocated various areas of settlement to the 12 tribes of Israel (including Ephraim and Manasseh, but none to Levi, the tribe of the priests). Nine-and-a-half tribes were on the west bank of the Jordan River, with two-and-a-half tribes on the east bank. In time, the east bank area that was north of Ammon came to be known as Gilead (Judges 11).

After Joshua died, the Israelite tribes attempted to maintain sovereignty over their own allotted territories in a loose tribal confederation.

While there was no designated national leader, various military heroes, known to us as "judges," were empowered by the Spirit of God to bring deliverance from Israel's enemies. In some cases the deliverance was local, while at other times the entire tribal confederacy benefitted. The data in the book of Judges gives a time span of 410 years. However, there were probably times when judgeships overlapped—that is, judges would be serving during the same time, but in different locations.[2] In addition, Jephthah's reference in Judges 11:26 to the passage of 300 years from Joshua (1406 BC) to himself (1105 BC) overlaps with the 480-year time span mentioned in 1 Kings 6:1, which goes from the exodus (1446 BC) to the fourth year of Solomon's reign (966 BC).

The main body of the story in the book of Judges revolves around six cycles of apostasy, distress, and deliverance. God intervened numerous times to deliver Israel from military oppression, spiritual depression, and physical annihilation, keeping His covenant promises and the messianic hope alive. The chart on the next page shows these six cycles.

The story of Judges ends in spiritual, moral, and social chaos (chapters 17–21). The only ray of light and hope during "the days of the judges" is the story of Ruth's commitment to Yahweh (Jehovah), the God of Israel. Her determination to follow Naomi to Bethlehem led to her eventual marriage to Boaz. Together they became the great-grandparents of David, who was destined to be Israel's greatest king (Ruth 4:13-22). The stage was now set for the arrival of the prophet Samuel, who would serve as the final link between the period of the judges and the kings of Israel.

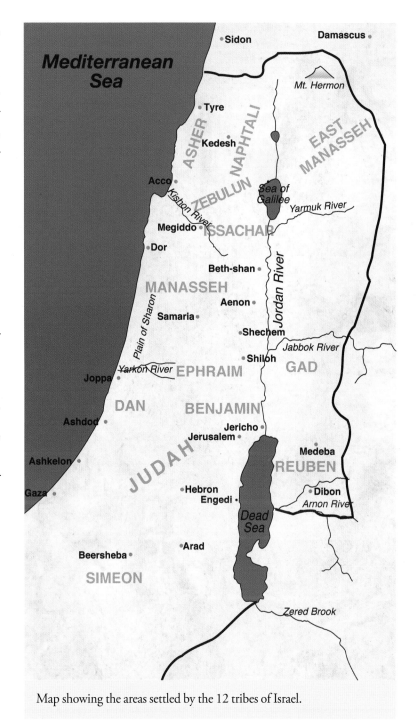

Map showing the areas settled by the 12 tribes of Israel.

Cycles in the Book of Judges

Cycle	Enemy	Period of Servitude	Judge	Period of Rest
First 3:7-11	Mesopotamia	8 Years (1381–1373 BC)	Othniel	40 years (1373–1334 BC)
Second 3:12-31	Moab	18 years (1334–1316 BC)	Ehud (Shamgar)	80 years (1316–1237 BC)
Third 4:1–5:31	Canaanites	20 years (1257–1237 BC)	Deborah and Barak	40 years (1191–1151 BC)
Fourth 6:1–8:32	Midianites	7 years (1198–1191 BC)	Gideon	40 years (1149–1105 BC)
Fifth 10:6–12:15	Ammonites (in the east)	18 years (1105–1087 BC)	Jephthah Ibzan Elon Abdon	31 years (1087–1058 BC)
Sixth 13:1–16:31	Philistines (in the west)	40 years	Samson	20 years (1069–1049 BC)

This chart by Ed Hindson, taken from Ed Hindson and Gary Yates's book *Essence of the Old Testament: A Survey* (Nashville, TN: B&H, 2012), 140. Used by permission.

Conquest and Chaos

(Joshua and Judges, Ruth)

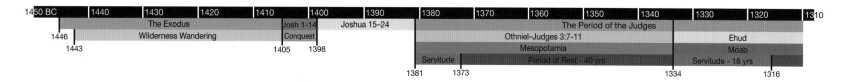

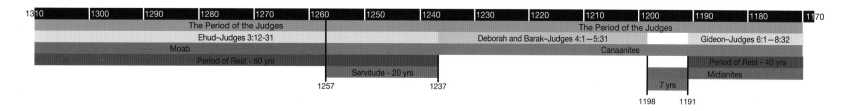

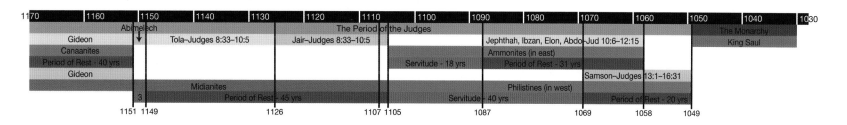

21

THE UNITED KINGDOM

AS THE PROPHET SAMUEL AGED, the people of Israel insisted they select a king "like all the nations" (1 Samuel 8:5). The Gentile nations had powerful, visible leaders, whereas Israel's king was the invisible God. The events surrounding Saul's selection as Israel's first king over the 12 tribes indicate that he was the people's choice, not God's. The people focused on Saul's appearance (1 Samuel 9:2) rather than his heart (1 Samuel 16:7). Though God permitted Saul's coronation, Samuel made it clear that the people had rejected God when they requested a human king (1 Samuel 10:19).

Saul's initial success rallied the 12-tribe alliance into a united nation. However, Saul's wrong choices and poor leadership caused his kingdom to deteriorate rapidly. Ultimately, his blatant disobedience against God's command to slay the Amalekites caused God to reject him as the king over Israel (1 Samuel 15:23).

Almost immediately the biblical text introduces David as the heir apparent and rightful future king with his victory over Goliath in the Valley of Elah (1 Samuel 17). Saul's jealousy of David led him to a murderous rage that eventually drove David and his men into hiding in

the wilderness for several years. As they fled from place to place, David continued to escape Saul's wrath. In the meantime, Saul wasted time and energy pursuing David while his real enemies grew stronger.

Tragically, Saul drove away the one man who could have really helped him. David was not present at the battle against the Philistines on Mount Gilboa, where Saul and his son Jonathan both died. Eventually David was anointed king over the tribe of Judah at Hebron when he was age 30 (2 Samuel 2:1-4). In the meantime, Saul's son Ishbosheth attempted to rule the ten northern tribes but was eventually assassinated by two of his own men. Afterward, the elders of the northern tribes came to Hebron and anointed David king over all Israel at age 37 (2 Samuel 5:1-4).

David's kingship was the great turning point for the nation and people of Israel. He quickly captured Jerusalem from the Jebusites and made it the capital of all Israel, eventually moving the Ark of the Covenant into the city. Under the promise of the Davidic Covenant (2 Samuel 7), David won military victories over Philistia, Moab, Ammon, Aram, and Edom. He extended Israel's borders from the river of Egypt to the Euphrates in partial fulfillment of God's promise to Abraham (Genesis 15:18). God promised David fame, land, rest, seed, a kingdom, a throne, and a dynasty forever (2 Samuel 7:9-16).

Despite David's sin with Bathsheba, the death of their first child, and the subsequent rebellion of Absalom, God's covenant with David was not nullified. The birth of Solomon ("peace"), also called Jedidiah ("loved by the Lord"), to David and Bathsheba indicated God's grace, forgiveness, and restoration based upon His covenant promises.

Urged by the prophet Nathan, David named Solomon to succeed him as king (1 Kings 1:1–2:12). Initially, God blessed Solomon greatly with wisdom, prosperity, and international fame. He not only continued to expand Israel's borders but engaged in massive building projects which included palaces, pools, stables, fortresses,

and ultimately the temple in Jerusalem (1 Kings 5–7). He oversaw the construction of the temple from the fourth to the eleventh year of his reign. The presence of God resided in His glory resting on the Ark of the Covenant in the Most Holy Place and assured the people of Israel that God was with them.

Unfortunately, as the years of peace and material prosperity continued, Solomon's heart was gradually lured away from God. His political marriages to foreign wives and his attempt to maintain peace with neighboring nations led him to accommodate other gods and pagan religious practices. Though Solomon held the 12 tribes under his control all through his long reign, as time went on, his empire began to disintegrate. With his death in 931 BC his enemies saw the opportunity to break away from the rule of the "house of David."

Map showing the boundaries of Israel during the reigns of Saul, David, and Solomon.

United Kingdom
(Samuel and Kings)

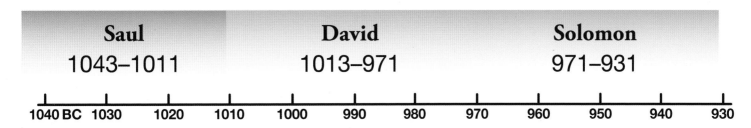

Saul	David	Solomon
1043–1011	1013–971	971–931

1040 BC 1030 1020 1010 1000 990 980 970 960 950 940 930

22

THE WISDOM BOOKS

THERE ARE FIVE WISDOM BOOKS in the Old Testament canon of Scripture: Job, Psalms, Proverbs, Ecclesiastes, and Song of Solomon. These books were written primarily by three human authors under the inspiration of the Holy Spirit—Job, David, and Solomon. The Psalms have multiple human authors, but David is the primary one.

Job was written by Job around 1650 BC and is not only the first of the wisdom books, but the oldest book in the entire Old Testament by about 200 years. Job is a prolegomenon to the entire Bible. In Job, in the life of a single individual, we see a microcosm of God's entire plan for history. Job loses his wealth and most of his family, as well as his own health, and experiences a great amount of suffering. Along the way, he has to endure the ungodly counsel of three supposed friends. However, at the end of his ordeal, God steps in and speaks and restores his health and gives him twice the wealth and family he had before. The book of Job deals with wisdom in relation to mankind's biggest problem, which is suffering. In a general sense, God is at work in history turning mankind's journey into sin around through Christ and

providing for the saved a much greater status for eternity than what was lost in Adam's fall.

Psalms is a book of worship specifically for Israel. It provides God's people with wisdom for worshipping Him, and the church has benefitted greatly from this material for its own worship of God.

Most of the psalms were penned by David, while others were written by Asaph, Korah, Solomon, Moses, Heman, and Ethan. There are even some psalms with anonymous writers. Most of the psalms were written around the time of King David, about 1025 BC. The book is commonly broken down into five segments:

> Book I—Psalms 1–41
>
> Book II—Psalms 42–72
>
> Book III—Psalms 73–89
>
> Book IV—Psalms 90–106
>
> Book V—Psalms 107–150

A great deal of theology is revealed in the Psalms; however, the main focus of the book as a whole is the praise of God. There are also different kinds of psalms that were used in connection with various occasions: messianic psalms, lament psalms, testimonial psalms, pilgrim psalms, imprecatory psalms, penitential psalms, wisdom psalms, historical psalms, nature psalms, and Torah psalms.

The final three wisdom books were written by King Solomon around 1000 BC. A Jewish tradition says that Solomon wrote the Song of Solomon early in his life when he was young, penned Proverbs in the middle of his life when he was mature and wise, then authored Ecclesiastes at the end of his life when he became apostate.

Even if this rabbinic statement is not true, there is no doubt that Solomon, said in the Bible to be the wisest man who ever lived, wrote these three books of wisdom. Proverbs provides wisdom (which in Hebrew means "skill in living") for everyday living. Ecclesiastes provides wisdom and insight into the evil of this world and where it leads. Worldly wisdom, labeled by Solomon as being "under the sun," always leads to vanity. Therefore, one does not have to learn this through experience; instead, a wise individual will take Solomon's word for where the things of this world lead. And finally, the Song of Solomon provides wisdom and insight into marital love and how to keep the fires of romance burning in the marriage relationship.

The Wisdom Books

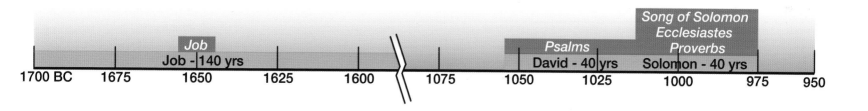

OLD TESTAMENT PROPHETS

THE MINISTRY OF THE PROPHETS is interspersed with the history of the kings of Israel and Judah. The Hebrew prophets proclaimed messages that were direct revelations from God. The books of prophecy (known as the "latter prophets" in the Hebrew Bible) were books of both preaching and predicting. The Word of the Lord was revealed to the prophets by the Holy Spirit and communicated to the people with powerful conviction and precise accuracy. Their messages were rooted in history but also extended into the future by means of predictive prophecy. Thus, the prophets spoke to their own generation through their preaching and to future generations through their predictions.

The English Bible includes five books commonly termed the Major Prophets and twelve books often called the Minor Prophets. The messages in these books remind us that God holds all nations accountable for their behavior and policies. He is the Lord of the universe before whom all nations must bow.

The themes of the Major Prophets are as follows:[1]

Themes of the Major Prophets	
Isaiah	God Is with Us
Jeremiah	The Babylonians Are Coming
Lamentations	Jerusalem Is Burning
Ezekiel	The Glory Will Return
Daniel	The Messiah Will Come

The Minor Prophets contain the twelve books from Hosea to Malachi and comprise the final section of the Old Testament. These books include twelve separate compositions in the English Bible, but they appear as a single "Book of the Twelve" in the Hebrew Bible. Their historical setting covers more than four centuries. Some of the books have clear chronological markers (for example, the names of kings) while others (such as Obadiah) do not and are more difficult to date.

The books of the Minor Prophets span the time from the Assyrian threat to the Babylonian captivity and beyond to the post-exilic return. Three of the minor prophets were focused on the Northern Kingdom of Israel (capital: Samaria).

Minor Prophets to the Northern Kingdom	
Prophet	Theme
Hosea	Unquenchable Love
Amos	Ultimate Justice
Jonah	Universal Concern

Six of the minor prophets were focused on the Southern Kingdom of Judah (capital: Jerusalem).

Minor Prophets to the Southern Kingdom	
Prophet	Theme
Joel	Day of the Lord
Obadiah	Doom of Edom
Micah	Divine Lawsuit
Nahum	Destruction of Nineveh
Habakkuk	Destruction of Babylon
Zephaniah	Disaster Is Imminent

The messages proclaimed by the prophets still speak to us today. They remind us that God holds all people responsible for their behavior. Thus, the call of the prophets echoes down the canyon of time, calling us to repent, believe, return, and experience God's grace today as well. Their message is one of hope for regeneration, revival, and restoration. They call not only their own generation to return to the Lord, but ultimately, every generation.

Most of the prophets can be clearly dated from their own writings. The prophet generally identifies *who* he is ("son of..."); *where* he is (e.g. "from Tekoa"); *when* he is ("during the reign of..."). From this information we can suggest the following dates:

March of the Prophets[2]	
Obadiah	850–840 BC
Joel	835–800 BC
Jonah	780–775 BC
Amos	c. 750 BC
Hosea	750–710 BC
Micah	740–710 BC
Isaiah	740–680 BC
Nahum	c. 650 BC
Zephaniah	635–625 BC
Habakkuk	615–605 BC
Ezekiel	590–570 BC
Jeremiah	610–570 BC
Lamentations	586 BC
Daniel	560–530 BC
Haggai	c. 520 BC
Zechariah	480–470 BC
Malachi	433–424 BC

The Old Testament Prophets

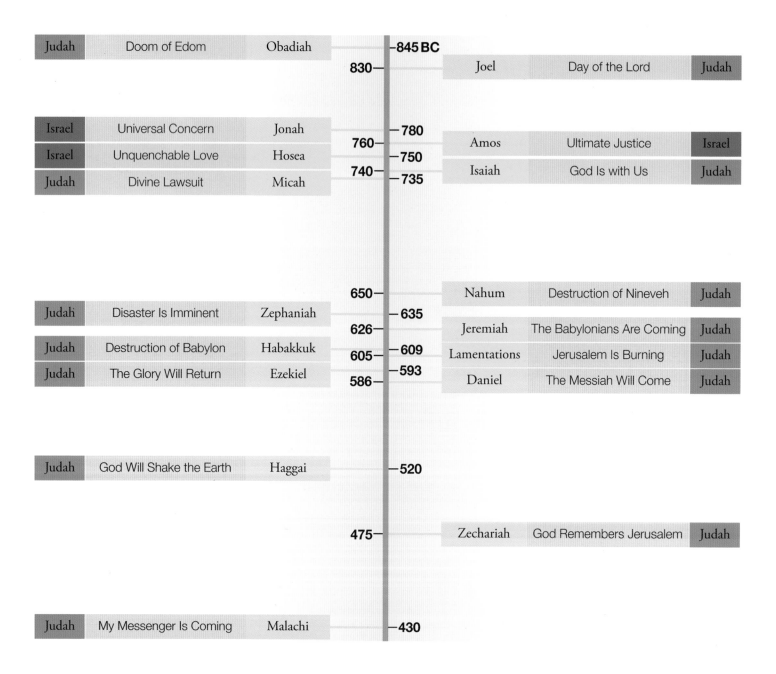

Judah	Doom of Edom	Obadiah		845 BC			
			830		Joel	Day of the Lord	Judah
Israel	Universal Concern	Jonah		780			
			760		Amos	Ultimate Justice	Israel
Israel	Unquenchable Love	Hosea		750			
			740	735	Isaiah	God Is with Us	Judah
Judah	Divine Lawsuit	Micah					
			650		Nahum	Destruction of Nineveh	Judah
Judah	Disaster Is Imminent	Zephaniah		635			
			626		Jeremiah	The Babylonians Are Coming	Judah
Judah	Destruction of Babylon	Habakkuk	605	609	Lamentations	Jerusalem Is Burning	Judah
Judah	The Glory Will Return	Ezekiel	586	593	Daniel	The Messiah Will Come	Judah
Judah	God Will Shake the Earth	Haggai		520			
			475		Zechariah	God Remembers Jerusalem	Judah
Judah	My Messenger Is Coming	Malachi		430			

THE KINGS OF ISRAEL AND JUDAH

THE BOOKS OF 1 AND 2 KINGS tell the story of the kings of Israel (Northern Kingdom) and Judah (Southern Kingdom) from the perspective of the Hebrew prophets. The parallel accounts in 1 and 2 Chronicles tell the same story from a priestly perspective. Together they provide an inspired record of Israel's history from the time of David until the Babylonian captivity.

In the books of 1 and 2 Kings, the various kings are elevated by the Mosaic (Deuteronomy 28) and Davidic (2 Samuel 7) Covenants. Whereas 1 Kings opens with the final days of David's reign and the glory of Solomon's rule, 2 Kings ends with the Lord's judgment on disobedient Israel. The books of 1 and 2 Kings present the outworking of both God's covenant promises and His discipline. Several prophets are introduced throughout the narrative, and they function as God's messengers to the kings and the people of Israel and Judah.

Each king is introduced in a consistent manner, with an introduction (name, age at accession, and family ancestry) followed by details about their accession, an evaluation, a historical record, the capital city of their reign, and a concluding reference (death, burial, duration of reign, and successor). By contrast, the prophets often appear on the scene in times of national crises without formal introduction.

In 931 BC, Solomon's son Rehoboam became the king of all Israel. However, a series of rash decisions by the young and inexperienced ruler led to the revolt of the northern tribes under Jeroboam. In the process, the Northern Kingdom rejected the line of David, the city of Jerusalem, and the temple, and eventually established its capital at Samaria under Omri. The Bible identifies all of the northern kings as ungodly and describes the Northern Kingdom's eventual destruction by the Assyrians in 722 BC.

In the meantime, the biblical record traces both the successes and failures of Judah's kings in the south. Some were great and godly leaders (such as Hezekiah), while others were just as evil and corrupt as their northern counterparts (for example, Ahaz). In Judah, there were times of revival and reform under men like Asa, Hezekiah, and Josiah. But ultimately the Southern Kingdom fell to the Babylonians in 586 BC.

The wickedness that proliferated under Manasseh's reign sealed

Map showing the Northern Kingdom of Israel and the Southern Kingdom of Judah.

Judah's eventual fate and set the nation on a disastrous course that the reforms implemented by Josiah could not fully reverse. Judah's covenant rebellion continued rapidly after Josiah's untimely death at the hands of Pharaoh Neco (2 Kings 23:28-30). Under Josiah's sons, conditions continued to deteriorate and the Babylonians attacked Jerusalem three times: 605 BC (Daniel), 597 BC (Ezekiel), and 586 BC (Jeremiah). Finally, in 586 BC, the Babylonians destroyed both Jerusalem and the temple. By this time, all Israel, both north and south, lay in ruins, and the people's hopes and dreams seemed crushed beneath the rubble. However, the books of Kings and Chronicles end on an optimistic note. The future was being kept alive by God's divine intervention—He would spare the Davidic line, thus maintaining the promise of the messianic hope (2 Kings 25:27-30; 2 Chronicles 36:22-23).

The accounts regarding the kings of Israel and Judah remind us of the frailty of human leadership. The great kingdom established by David and Solomon was quickly demolished by a series of corrupt leaders who fell under God's judgment rather than experiencing His blessing. Their stories remind us of the importance of obedience in our own lives if we desire to know God's blessings.

The following charts survey the history of the kings of Israel and Judah based on the charts by Andrew Woods in Ed Hindson and Gary Yates's book *Essence of the Old Testament: A Survey* (Nashville, TN: B&H, 2012), 174-76. Used by permission.

Kings of Israel

King	Lineage	Scripture	Years of reign	Dates of reign (Thiele)	Co regency	Character	Prophet
Jeroboam I	Son of Nebat	1 Kgs 11:26–14:20	22	931–910		Bad	Ahijah, man of God from Judah, old prophet at Bethel, Iddo
Nadab	Son of Jeroboam I	1 Kgs 15:25-28	2	910–909		Bad	
Baasha	Son of Ahijah	1 Kgs 15:27–16:7	24	909–886		Bad	Jehu

Kings of Israel (continued)

King	Lineage	Scripture	Years of reign	Dates of reign (Thiele)	Co regency	Character	Prophet
Elah	Son of Baasha	1 Kgs 16:6-14	2	886–885		Bad	
Zimri	Chariot commander under Elah	1 Kgs 6:9-20	7 days	885		Bad	
Omri	Army commander under Elah	1 Kgs 6:15-28	12	885–874		Bad	
Ahab	Son of Omri	1 Kgs 16:28–22:40	22	874–853		Bad	Elijah, Elisha, Micaiah, unnamed prophets
Ahaziah	Son of Ahab	1 Kgs 22:40–2 Kgs 1:18	2	853–852		Bad	Elijah, Elisha
Joram	Son of Ahab	2 Kgs 1:17–9:26	12	852–841		Bad	Elisha
Jehu	Son of Nimishi; army commander under Ahab	2 Kgs 9:1–10:36	28	841–814		Bad	Elisha
Jehoahaz	Son of Jehu	2 Kgs 13:1-9	17	814–798		Bad	Elisha
Jehoash	Son of Jehoahaz	2 Kgs 13:10–14:16	16	798–782	Yes	Bad	Elisha

Kings of Israel (continued)

King	Lineage	Scripture	Years of reign	Dates of reign (Thiele)	Co regency	Character	Prophet
Jeroboam II	Son of Jehoash	2 Kgs 14:23-29	41	793–753	Yes	Bad	Jonah, Amos, Hosea
Zechariah	Son of Jeroboam II	2 Kgs 14:29–15:12	6 months	753–752		Bad	Hosea
Shallum	Son of Jabesh	2 Kgs 15:10-15	1 month	752		Bad	Hosea
Menahem	Son of Gadi	2 Kgs 15:14-22	10	752–742	Yes	Bad	Hosea
Pekahiah	Son of Menahem	2 Kgs 15:22-26	2	742–740		Bad	Hosea
Pekah	Son of Remaliah	2 Kgs 15:25-31	20	752–732	Yes	Bad	Hosea, Obed
Hoshea	Son of Elah	2 Kgs 15:30–17:6	9	732–722		Bad	Hosea

Kings of Judah

King	Lineage	Scripture	Years of reign	Dates of reign (Thiele)	Co regency	Character	Prophet
Rehoboam	Son of Solomon	1 Kgs 11:42–14:31	17	931–913		Bad	Shemiah, Iddo
Abijam	Son of Rehoboam	1 Kgs 14:31–15:8	3	913–911		Bad	Iddo
Asa	Son of Abijam	1 Kgs 15:8-24	41	911–870		Good	Azariah, Obed, Hanani
Jehoshaphat	Son of Asa	1 Kgs 22:41-50	25	870–848	Yes	Good	Jehu, Jahaziel, Eliezer
Jehoram	Son of Jehoshaphat	2 Kgs 8:16-24	8	848–841	Yes	Bad	Obadiah, Elijah
Ahaziah	Son of Jehoram	2 Kgs 8:24–9:29	1	841		Bad	
Athlaiah	Daughter of Ahab	2 Kgs 11:1-20	6	841–835		Bad	
Joash		2 Kgs 11:1–12:21	40	835–796		Good	Joel
Amaziah	Son of Joash	2 Kgs 14:1-20	29	796–767		Good	Unnamed prophets
Uzziah	Son of Amaziah	2 Kgs 14:21; 15:1-7	52	767–740	Yes	Good	Isaiah, Zechariah

Kings of Judah (continued)

King	Lineage	Scripture	Years of reign	Dates of reign (Thiele)	Co regency	Character	Prophet
Jotham	Son of Uzziah	2 Kgs 15:32-38	16	740–732	Yes	Good	Isaiah, Micah
Ahaz	Son of Jotham	2 Kgs 16:1-20	16	732–716	Yes	Bad	Isaiah, Micah
Hezekiah	Son of Ahaz	2 Kgs 18:1–20:21	29	716–687	Yes	Good	Isaiah, Micah
Manasseh	Son of Hezekiah	2 Kgs 21:1-18	55	687–642	Yes	Bad	Nahum, unnamed prophets
Amon	Son of Manasseh	2 Kgs 21:19-26	2	642–640		Bad	
Josiah	Son of Amon	2 Kgs 21:26–23:30	31	640–608		Good	Jeremiah, Zephaniah, Huldah
Jehoahaz	Son of Josiah	2 Kgs 23:30-33	3 months	608		Bad	Jeremiah
Jehoiakim	Son of Josiah	2 Kgs 23:34–24:5	11	608–597		Bad	Jeremiah, Habakkuk, Daniel, Uriah
Jehoiachin	Son of Jehoiakim	2 Kgs 24:6-16; 25:27-30	3 months	597		Bad	Jeremiah, Daniel
Zedekiah	Son of Josiah	2 Kgs 24:17–25:7	11	597–586		Bad	Jeremiah, Daniel, Ezekiel

The Kings of Israel and Judah
(1 and 2 Kings)

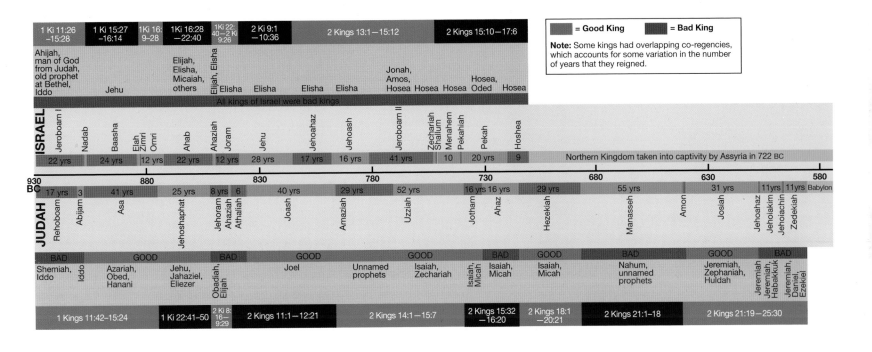

| 1 Ki 11:26 –15:28 | 1 Ki 15:27 –16:14 | 1Ki 16: 9–28 | 1Ki 16:28 –22:40 | 1Ki 22: 40—2 Ki 9:26 | 2 Ki 9:1 –10:36 | 2 Kings 13:1—15:12 | 2 Kings 15:10—17:6 |

= Good King **= Bad King**

Note: Some kings had overlapping co-regencies, which accounts for some variation in the number of years that they reigned.

Ahijah, man of God from Judah, old prophet at Bethel, Iddo

Jehu

Elijah, Elisha, Micaiah, others

Elijah, Elisha

Elisha   Elisha   Elisha   Elisha

Jonah, Amos, Hosea   Hosea   Hosea

Hosea, Oded   Hosea

All kings of Israel were bad kings

ISRAEL

Jeroboam I | Nadab | Baasha | Elah Zimri Omri | Ahab | Ahaziah Joram | Jehu | Jehoahaz | Jehoash | Jeroboam II | Zechariah Shallum Menahem Pekahiah | Pekah | Hoshea

22 yrs | 24 yrs | 12 yrs | 22 yrs | 12 yrs | 28 yrs | 17 yrs | 16 yrs | 41 yrs | 10 | 20 yrs | 9

Northern Kingdom taken into captivity by Assyria in 722 BC

930 BC | 880 | 830 | 780 | 730 | 680 | 630 | 580 Babylon

17 yrs | 3 | 41 yrs | 25 yrs | 8 yrs | 6 | 40 yrs | 29 yrs | 52 yrs | 16 yrs 16 yrs | 29 yrs | 55 yrs | 31 yrs | 11yrs | 11yrs

JUDAH

Rehoboam | Abijam | Asa | Jehoshaphat | Jehoram Ahaziah Athaliah | Joash | Amaziah | Uzziah | Jotham Ahaz | Hezekiah | Manasseh | Amon | Josiah | Jehoahaz Jehoiakim Jehoiachin Zedekiah

BAD | GOOD | BAD | GOOD | GOOD | BAD | GOOD | BAD | GOOD | BAD

Shemiah, Iddo | Iddo | Azariah, Obed, Hanani | Jehu, Jahaziel, Eliezer | Obadiah, Elijah | Joel | Unnamed prophets | Isaiah, Zechariah | Isaiah, Micah | Isaiah, Micah | Isaiah, Micah | Nahum, unnamed prophets | Jeremiah, Zephaniah, Huldah | Jeremiah, Jeremiah, Habakkuk | Jeremiah, Daniel, Ezekiel

| 1 Kings 11:42–15:24 | 1 Ki 22:41–50 | 2 Ki 8: 16— 9:29 | 2 Kings 11:1–12:21 | 2 Kings 14:1—15:7 | 2 Kings 15:32 —16:20 | 2 Kings 18:1 —20:21 | 2 Kings 21:1–18 | 2 Kings 21:19—25:30 |

25

THE BABYLONIAN CAPTIVITY

BABYLON IS THE SECOND-MOST-FREQUENTLY mentioned city in the entire Bible, about 350 times, next to Jerusalem. The kingdom of man began with the Tower of Babel event in Genesis 11. God responded in Genesis 12 with the call of Abraham and the launching of His counter-kingdom—the kingdom of God—with His city as Jerusalem. That is why God used His arch-enemy Babylon to discipline His people in Judah, or the Southern Kingdom of Israel. Then after the 70-year captivity was completed, God providentially made it possible for the people of Judah to return to their land—unlike the people of the Northern Kingdom, who remained in captivity and ended up becoming scattered throughout the nations.

We know from the beginning of chapter 9 (verse 2) that Daniel had read about "the number of years which was revealed as the word of the LORD to Jeremiah the prophet for the completion of the desolations of Jerusalem, namely, seventy years." The two passages which Daniel surely studied were Jeremiah 25:11-12 and 29:10-14.

"This whole land shall be a desolation and a horror, and these nations shall serve the king of Babylon seventy years. Then it will be when seventy years are completed I will punish the king of Babylon and that nation," declares the LORD, "for their iniquity, and the land of the Chaldeans; and I will make it an everlasting desolation" (Jeremiah 25:11-12).

For thus says the LORD, "When seventy years have been completed for Babylon, I will visit you and fulfill My good word to you, to bring you back to this place. For I know the plans that I have for you," declares the LORD, "plans for welfare and not for calamity to give you a future and a hope. Then you will call upon Me and come and pray to Me, and I will listen to you. And you will seek Me and find Me when you search for Me with all your heart. I will be found by you," declares the LORD, "and I will restore your fortunes and will gather you from all the nations and from all the places where I have driven you," declares the LORD, "and I will bring you back to the place from where I sent you into exile" (Jeremiah 29:10-14).

The Babylonian Captivity

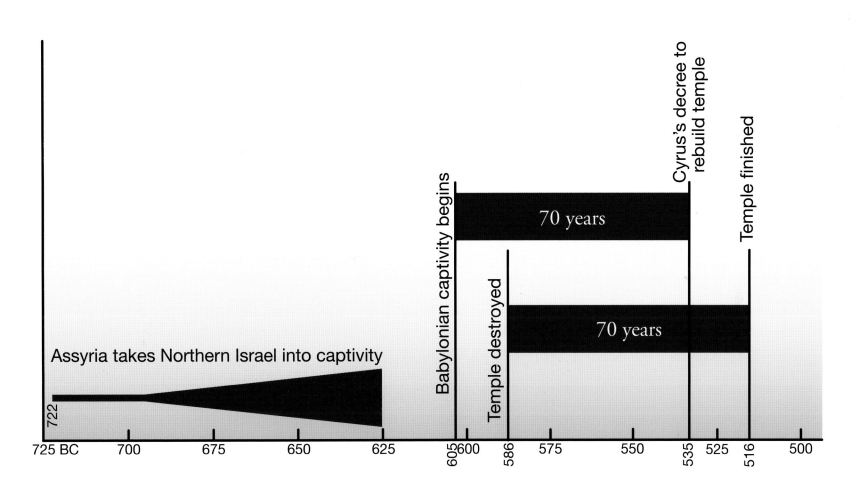

722

725 BC   700   675   650   625   605 600   586   575   550   535   525   516   500

Assyria takes Northern Israel into captivity

Babylonian captivity begins

Temple destroyed

Cyrus's decree to rebuild temple

Temple finished

70 years

70 years

Both texts clearly speak of Israel's Babylonian captivity as limited to a 70-year period. Both passages also blend into their texts statements that look forward to a time of ultimate fulfillment and blessing for the nation of Israel. That is why Daniel appears to think that when the people return to their land, then ultimate blessing (the millennial kingdom) will coincide with their return. Daniel's errant thinking about the timing of God's plan for Israel occasioned the Lord's sending of Gabriel "to give you insight with understanding" (Daniel 9:22).

In the historical books of Samuel, Kings, and Chronicles, the Lord provided a divine commentary to the nation on how it was keeping or not keeping His Law. And in 2 Chronicles 36:20-21, the Lord explained why He ended up sending the people away to Babylon for 70 years:

> Those who had escaped from the sword he carried away to Babylon; and they were servants to him and to his sons until the rule of the kingdom of Persia, to fulfill the word of the LORD by the mouth of Jeremiah, until the land had enjoyed its sabbaths. All the days of its desolation it kept sabbath until seventy years were complete (2 Chronicles 36:20-21).

It is clear from the above passages that God had a specific reason behind the deportation of the Southern Kingdom (Judah) to Babylon for 70 years. Keep in mind that the Jews entered the Promised Land around 1400 BC, and were deported to Babylon around 600 BC. This means that they were in the land for about 800 years before the Babylonian deportation. Had they disobeyed the sabbatical year commandment every seventh year, that would mean they should have been in captivity for about 114 years. Instead, they were held captive for 70 years, meaning that they were disobedient for only 490 of the 800 years in the land. This would mean that there were breaks or gaps in the accumulation of the 490 years during the 800-year period. Why is this important? Because many of the critics of the literal interpretation of the 70-weeks prophecy in Daniel 9:24-27 insist that it is unreasonable to have gaps in that 490-year period. But it's not, for there were multiple gaps in the 490-year period related to the Babylonian captivity.

The Northern Kingdom was taken away into captivity by the Assyrians in 721 BC and never officially returned. Judah was first taken into captivity during a three-stage process. The first phase took place in 606 BC, when Daniel and others were taken to Babylon and entered into the king of Babylon's service (Isaiah 39:3-8; Daniel 1:3-4; 2 Chronicles 36:6-7). The second phase was in 597 BC, when both King Johoiachin and Ezekiel, along with many others, were taken to Babylon (2 Kings 24:10-16). By this time, only the poorest of people remained in the land of Judah (2 Kings 24:16). The third and final phase took place in 586 BC, when Judah's last king, Zedekiah, was carried away. This time, the walls of Jerusalem were destroyed and both the temple and the city were burned (2 Kings 25:1-7).

Scripture, then, speaks of two 70-year periods. The first ran from 606 to 536 BC and had to do with the 70-year Babylonian captivity (Jeremiah 29:10). The second began in 586 BC and ended when the Second Temple was finished in 516 BC (Ezra 6:13-15). The number of Jews who returned to the land of Israel was about 50,000 (Ezra 2:64-65). After the Babylonian captivity was over, a godly remnant returned to the land, repented of their past sins, and made an effort to serve the Lord and obey His covenant (Ezra 9–10).

26

DANIEL'S PROPHETIC TIMELINE

D ANIEL IS ONE OF THE MOST important books of the Bible with regard to the chronology of future events because it provides a great amount of key information about the players and time sequences of end-time prophecy. Daniel introduced much of what the New Testament book of Revelation accepted and expanded upon. Thus, Daniel is the fountainhead out of which springs the major themes of Bible prophecy. It is impossible to understand prophecy and biblical chronology without looking to the book of Daniel.

In Daniel we find graphic visions that provide an outline of what God would do from the sixth century BC—when Daniel lived and wrote—until the coming of Messiah's kingdom in the Millennium. The key prophetic and chronological chapters are Daniel 2, 7, 9, 11, and 12. And chapters 2, 7, and 9 provide broad outlines for Jewish and Gentile history.

While the nation of Israel was captive in Babylon, God provided Daniel and the people with an outline and chronological framework for their history. He did this to give them hope and to confirm that He had a plan for their future.

More specifically, Daniel chapters 2 and 7 provide a panoramic overview of four Gentile kingdoms that would play important roles in world history. The first of the four kingdoms was Babylon, under whose jurisdiction Daniel saw and wrote many of his prophetic visions. The other kingdoms were Medo-Persia, Greece, and Rome.

Daniel concluded these overviews by saying that the lands that made up the former Roman Empire would undergo a revival in the form of a ten-nation confederacy immediately before the coming of Messiah's kingdom. Daniel 2 presents these kingdoms from a Gentile perspective, while Daniel 7 presents them from God's perspective, which explains why the kingdoms are characterized as beasts. When man's fallen sinful nature is not restrained, especially when placed in a position of rule over other people, then it manifests itself as having the characteristics of a wild animal that is out of control.

Daniel chapters 11 and 12 also provide information that's essential for understanding Bible prophecy. For example, Daniel 11 gives many details relating to the Antichrist. Daniel 12 provides further chronological details about the Tribulation and lets us know that there will be an interval of 75 days between Christ's second coming and the beginning of the Millennium.

Central to Daniel's prophetic visions are the four Gentile kingdoms that appear as different parts of a statue in Daniel 2 and as different kinds of beasts in Daniel 7. These four entities make up various kingdoms of man, which are all set in opposition to God's kingdom.

The four kingdoms are first revealed in Daniel 2:29-35. There, we read about a dream Nebuchadnezzar had, in which he saw a large statue of a man whose body parts were comprised of different metals. The head was of gold, the chest area and arms were of silver, the hips and thighs were made of bronze, the legs were made of iron, and the feet were comprised of part iron and part baked clay. In verses 36-45, Daniel explained the meaning of this dream to Nebuchadnezzar. He pointed out that history would be dominated by four powerful Gentile kingdoms that would rule the world until they were destroyed by the fifth and final kingdom, God's kingdom involving national Israel. This period of Gentile domination, which started with the rise of Babylon in 612 BC, is called "the times of the Gentiles" (Luke 21:24).

Here are some specifics about the four kingdoms as revealed in Daniel chapters 2 and 7:

- *Babylon* (612–539 BC)—represented by the head of gold (2:32) and a lion having the wings of an eagle (7:4)

- *Medo-Persia* (539–331 BC)—represented by the upper body of silver (2:32) and a bear (7:5)

- *Greece* (331–63 BC)—represented by the belly and thighs made of bronze (2:32) and a leopard with four wings and four heads (7:6)

- *Rome* (63 BC–AD 476; the Tribulation)—the first phase of this kingdom is represented by legs of iron (2:33) and an unspecified beast with iron teeth and bronze claws (7:7); the final phase is described as feet and toes that are a mixture of iron and clay (2:41-43), as well as ten horns or ten kings and "another" (7:24-25)

The first three kingdoms and the first phase of the fourth kingdom are all past. What still remains future is the second phase of the fourth kingdom, or the revived Roman Empire. Daniel 7 speaks of the rise of a ten-horned phase of the fourth kingdom, which represents the Antichrist's kingdom during the Tribulation (7:20-28). One of the horns is called "the little horn" (7:8), who is the Antichrist. He will rise up and dominate the ten-nation confederacy (or revised Roman Empire), and from there he will eventually go on to rule the world (7:23).

The book of Revelation builds upon the prophetic details given in Daniel and further develops the final phase of the fourth kingdom, or Antichrist's rule. Dr. John Walvoord made this observation:

> The minute description given here of the end time, the fourth beast, and the ten horns followed by the eleventh horn that gained control of three has never been fulfilled in history. Some expositors have attempted to find ten kings of the past and the eleventh king who would arise to somehow fulfill this prophecy, but there is nothing corresponding to this in the history of the Roman Empire. The ten horns do not reign one after the other, but they reign simultaneously. Further, they were not the world empire, but they were the forerunner to the little horn which after subduing three of the ten horns will go on to become a world ruler (v. 23; Revelation 13:7).[1]

The Antichrist will rise up within the revived Roman Empire, or a ten-nation confederacy in Europe, and eventually he will establish a one-world government.

Daniel 9:24-27 is one of the most chronologically important passages in the Bible (for more details, see chapter 27, "The 70 Weeks of Daniel"). The prophecy in this passage predicts the very day when the Messiah would ride into Jerusalem on a donkey in an event known as "the Triumphal Entry" (Luke 19:41-44). With this appearance, Christ fulfilled the first 69 weeks of years, or 483 years (Daniel 9:26), in this prophecy. The final week of years, or 7 years, will be fulfilled with the arrival of the Tribulation (Daniel 9:27).

Daniel's Prophetic Timeline
(Daniel 2, 7, 9–12)

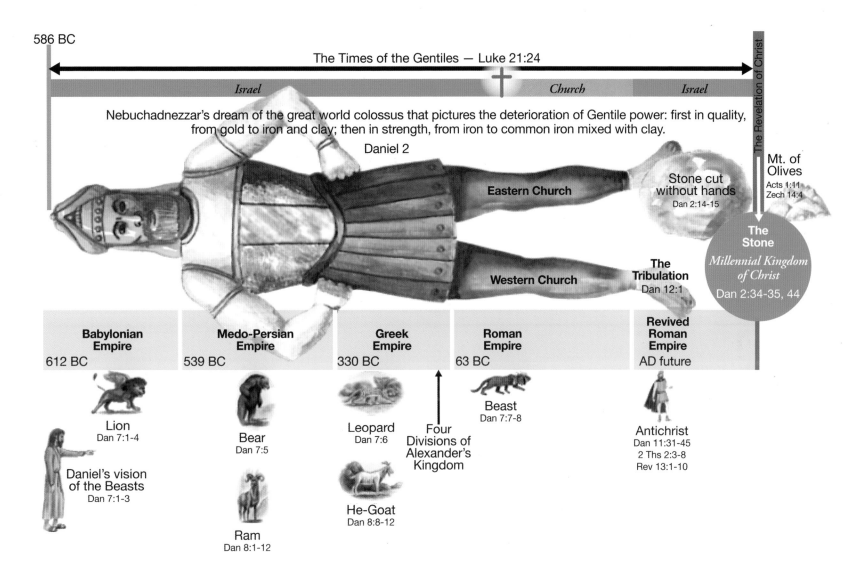

586 BC

The Times of the Gentiles — Luke 21:24

Israel   *Church*   *Israel*

The Revelation of Christ

Nebuchadnezzar's dream of the great world colossus that pictures the deterioration of Gentile power: first in quality, from gold to iron and clay; then in strength, from iron to common iron mixed with clay.

Daniel 2

Eastern Church

Stone cut without hands
Dan 2:14-15

Mt. of Olives
Acts 1:11
Zech 14:4

Western Church

The Tribulation
Dan 12:1

The Stone
Millennial Kingdom of Christ
Dan 2:34-35, 44

Babylonian Empire	**Medo-Persian Empire**	**Greek Empire**	**Roman Empire**	**Revived Roman Empire**
612 BC	539 BC	330 BC	63 BC	AD future

Lion
Dan 7:1-4

Daniel's vision of the Beasts
Dan 7:1-3

Bear
Dan 7:5

Ram
Dan 8:1-12

Leopard
Dan 7:6

He-Goat
Dan 8:8-12

Four Divisions of Alexander's Kingdom

Beast
Dan 7:7-8

Antichrist
Dan 11:31-45
2 Ths 2:3-8
Rev 13:1-10

27

THE 70 WEEKS OF DANIEL

DANIEL'S "70 WEEKS" PROPHECY, proclaimed in Daniel 9:24-27, is the framework within which the 7-year Tribulation (or the 70th week) occurs. The prophecy of the 70 weeks of years was given to Daniel by God through the angel Gabriel during the Babylonian captivity (Daniel 9:1; 2 Chronicles 36:21-23; Ezra 1; 6:3-5). Daniel was concerned for his people, who were nearing the end of their 70-year captivity. In Daniel's vision, he was reassured that God had not forgotten His chosen people. The angel Gabriel told Daniel that God would bring the people of Israel back into their land and would one day set up the messianic kingdom. What Daniel didn't expect was the revelation that this prophecy would not be fulfilled at the end of the 70-year captivity in Babylon, but at the end of the future 70 weeks of years described in Daniel 9:24-27. There, we read that the Antichrist will emerge in power during the prophetic milestone known as the 70th week:

> He [the Antichrist] will make a firm covenant with the many for one week, but in the middle of the week he will put a stop to sacrifice and grain offering; and on the wing of abominations will come one who makes desolate, even until a complete destruction, one that is decreed, is poured out on the one who makes desolate (verse 27).

This 70th week, a future 7-year period, is also known as the Tribulation. This era will follow the rapture of the church and will be a time of unparalleled suffering and turmoil. A wide variety of descriptive terms are used in Scripture to speak of this 7-year period: Tribulation, Great Tribulation, Day of the Lord, day of wrath, day of distress, day of trouble, Time of Jacob's Trouble, day of darkness and gloom, and wrath of the Lamb.

At the beginning of the second half of the seventieth week (the 70th "seven"), the Antichrist will break the covenant he made with Israel. It will remain broken for three-and-a-half years, or "time, times, and half a time" (Daniel 7:25; 12:7; Revelation 12:14). And because the first 69 weeks (69 "sevens") were fulfilled literally, we can expect the 70th "seven," which is yet unfulfilled, to be fulfilled literally as well.

Explanation of Daniel's 70 Weeks of Years

69 x 7 x 360 = 173,880 days

March 5, 444 BC + 173,880 = March 30, AD 33

Verification

444 BC to AD 33 = 476 years

476 years x 365.2421989 days =	173,855 days
+ days between March 5 and March 30 =	25 days
Total =	173,880 days

Rationale for 360-Day Years

1/2 week—Daniel 9:27

Time, times, and half a time—Daniel 7:25; 12:7; Revelation 12:14

1260 days—Revelation 11:3; 12:6

42 months—Revelation 11:2; 13:5

Thus: 42 months = 1260 days = time, times, half a time = 1/2 week

Therefore: month = 30 days; year = 360 days[1]

Textual Reasons for a Gap

A careful reading of the text in Daniel indicates support for the idea that there is a gap of time between the 69th and 70th weeks in Daniel's prophecy. Note that the text says, "Then after the sixty-two weeks…"—in other words, after the 7 plus 62 weeks, which equals a total of 69 weeks of years (483 years total). The Hebrew text uses a conjunction combined with a preposition, usually translated "and after," or better, "then after" (NASB). "It is the only indication given regarding the chronological relation between these sixty-two weeks and the cutting off of the Anointed One. This event will occur 'after' their close, but nothing is said as to how long after."[2]

Robert Culver clearly states the implication of what this text says:

> There can be no honest difference of opinion about that: the cutting off of Messiah is "after" the sixty-two weeks. It

is not the concluding event of the series of sixty-two weeks. Neither is it said to be the opening event of the seventieth. It is simply after the seven plus sixty-two weeks.[3]

Steven Miller, in his commentary on Daniel, summarizes developments in the passage thus far as follows:

> After the reconstruction of Jerusalem in the first seven sevens (forty-nine years), another "sixty-two sevens" (434 years) would pass. Then two momentous events would take place. First, the "Anointed One" would come (v. 25), then he would be "cut off." Apparently his coming would be immediately at the end of the sixty-nine sevens…"[4]

There is no real debate among conservative interpreters as to who is spoken of by the phrase "the Messiah will be cut off." This refers to the crucifixion of Christ, which occurred four days later. Thus, it means that Jesus would be crucified after the 7 and 62 weeks, but before the beginning of the 70th week mentioned in the next verse (9:27). For this to take place requires a gap of time between the 69th and 70th weeks. This is not the result of an *a priori* belief like dispensationalism, as claimed by some. G.H. Lang notes, "It is here that the interval in the Seventy Sevens must fall. This is not a matter of inference, but of fact."[5] There is no other way to put this material together into a chronological sequence than to see the fulfillment of the 70th week as taking place in the future.

The passage also tells us that after the death of Christ, He will "have nothing." To what does this phrase refer? Surely it points to something already mentioned in the passage, and seems to refer to the six purpose clauses in verse 24, which are said to be the goal of the prophecy for Daniel's people and city. Therefore, if these clauses are to be fulfilled for Israel and Jerusalem in the same way the earlier parts of the passage were fulfilled (since they obviously did not occur in the past), they must take place at a time future even to our own day.

Verse 26 then goes on to describe the destruction of Jerusalem and the temple, which took place in AD 70. No matter how anyone figures it, these events cannot fit into the remaining 7 years of verse 27. There were at least 37 years between the death of Christ and the

The 70 Weeks of Daniel
(Daniel 9:24-27)

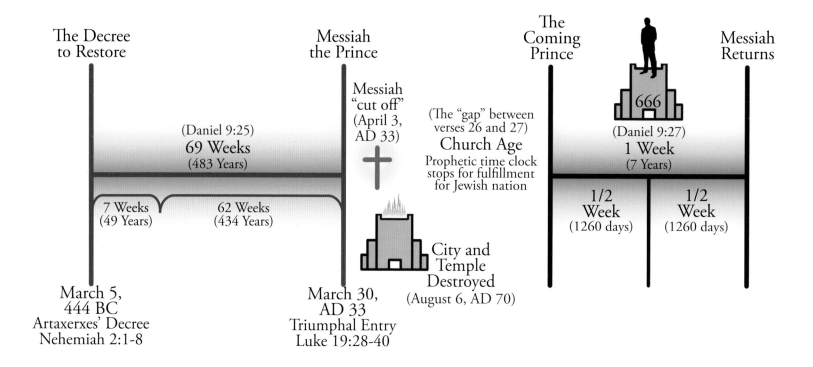

The Decree to Restore

Messiah the Prince

The Coming Prince

Messiah Returns

Messiah "cut off" (April 3, AD 33)

(Daniel 9:25)
69 Weeks
(483 Years)

(The "gap" between verses 26 and 27)
Church Age
Prophetic time clock stops for fulfillment for Jewish nation

666

(Daniel 9:27)
1 Week
(7 Years)

7 Weeks (49 Years)

62 Weeks (434 Years)

1/2 Week (1260 days)

1/2 Week (1260 days)

City and Temple Destroyed
(August 6, AD 70)

March 5, 444 BC
Artaxerxes' Decree
Nehemiah 2:1-8

March 30, AD 33
Triumphal Entry
Luke 19:28-40

destruction of Jerusalem. How is it possible for the events of the 70th week to have unfolded right after the crucifixion? It's not. However, the literal postponement view, which allows for a gap between weeks 69 and 70, allows things to fit very nicely because both Christ's death and the AD 70 destruction of Jerusalem occurred after the end of the 483-year period. Randall Price, when speaking of the events mentioned in verse 26, notes the following:

> "The cutting off of Messiah," and of "the people of the prince," are stated to occur after the sixty-nine weeks. If this was intended to occur in the seventieth week, the text

would have read here "during" or "in the midst of" (cf. Daniel's use of *hetzi*, "in the middle of," verse 27). This language implies that these events precede the seventieth week, but do not immediately follow the sixty-ninth. Therefore, a temporal interval separates the two.[6]

Only the literal, futurist understanding of the 70 weeks of Daniel can permit, in a precise manner, a sensible interpretation of this passage.

A further problem with the continuous fulfillment view is that its proponents have to jam the events of verses 26 and 27 into a single week of years, or one 7-year period. However, verse 27 speaks specifically about what will occur during the 70th week of years, and it does *not* include anything from verse 26. This is another textual basis for postponing the fulfillment of the 70th week into the future.

In summary, why does Daniel 9:27 support a gap between the 69th and 70th weeks? None of the events specifically said to occur during the 70th week have yet taken place. Also, continuous fulfillment advocates must make the 7-year covenant mentioned in verse 27 be a covenant between Christ and the church, when in reality it will be made between Antichrist and the nation of Israel. Because this covenant will be broken at the midpoint of the week (that is, after three-and-a-half years), their view means that Christ made a covenant that He will then break.

However, Christ did not make such a covenant at His first coming. What's more, would it make sense for Jesus to make a covenant, then simply break it at any time He wants? The language of verse 27 simply does not fit what we know of Christ's first coming, as clearly recorded in the Gospels.

Because a week of years is a 7-year period, the middle of a week of years would be three-and-a-half years into the 7-year period.

Interestingly, Daniel 7:25 and 12:7 both refer to a three-and-a-half year period (time, times, and half a time). In both passages, the context speaks of a future time involving the beast or the Antichrist. This would support a futurist understanding of the 70th week.

Daniel 7:25 says, "He [the Antichrist] will speak out against the Most High and wear down the saints of the Highest One, and he will intend to make alterations in times and in law; and they will be given into his hand for a time, times, and half a time." While this passage was given to Daniel before he received the revelation in chapter 9, it seems clear that the logic for the chronology of Daniel 7:25 is drawn from the 70-weeks prophecy of chapter 9. Daniel 12:7 reads, "I heard the man dressed in linen, who was above the waters of the river, as he raised his right hand and his left toward heaven, and swore by Him who lives forever that it would be for a time, times, and half a time; and as soon as they finish shattering the power of the holy people, all these events will be completed."

Both Daniel 9:27 and 12:7 speak of the Antichrist's rule coming to an end at the conclusion of the same three-and-a-half year period. This supports the notion that they both refer to a yet future time that we often call the Great Tribulation.

28

THE INTERTESTAMENTAL PERIOD

A S THE OLD TESTAMENT CLOSES, the Persians are ruling over Israel. They have allowed the Jews to return to the Promised Land and to build the Second Temple. But when the New Testament begins, the Romans are ruling the world. In between the testaments is a period of about 400 years, often referred to as the Intertestamental Period, which can be divided into four sections:

Late Persian Period	400–323 BC
Greek Period	323–167 BC
Period of Independence	167–63 BC
Roman Period	63 BC–AD 325

Many of the Apocryphal books were written during this period of time. While they contain errors and false teachings, some of these books (such as 1–2 Maccabees) do provide factual information about the Intertestamental Period, especially in relation to the Maccabean revolt against the Hellenistic overlords led by Antiochus IV Epiphanes.

Greek Period

During the late Persian period the Jews enjoyed a time of relative peace and prosperity. However, tensions between the Greeks from the west and Persians from the east led to inevitable conflict between the two superpowers (see Daniel 8:1-14). In 333 BC, Alexander the Great, at the age of 21, set out to destroy Persia and take over the Middle East. By 331 BC, Alexander conquered all the territory from Asia Minor to Egypt (including Judah and Jerusalem) to Persepolis in Persia (modern-day Iran). In the course of this conquest, Alexander founded Greek cities and colonies (such as Alexandria, Egypt) and spread the Greek language as the international tongue from Athens to India. Despite the later conquest by the Latin-speaking Romans, Greek remained the primary written language on into the New Testament era, which is why the books of the New Testament were written in Greek.

Following Alexander's death in Babylon at age 33 in 323 BC, his generals divided the Hellenistic empire into four basic regions: Greece (*Hellas*), Macedonia, Egypt, and Babylonia (Daniel 7:6; 8:8). In time,

Kings of North and South

NORTH: Seleucids		SOUTH: Ptolemies	
Seleucid I 312–280 BC	Founded Antioch	Ptolemy I Soter 323–285 BC	Established the Library at Alexandria
Antiochus I 280–261 BC	War with Ptolemies	Ptolemy II Philadelphus 285–246 BC	Septuagint
Antiochus II 261–246 BC	War with Ptolemies	Ptolemy III Euregetes 246–221 BC	War with Seleucids
Seleucus II 246–223 BC		Ptolemy IV Philopater	Defeated Seleucids at Raphia in 217 BC
Antiochus III The Great 223–187 BC	Conquered Israel in 200 BC	Ptolemy V Epiphanes 203–181 BC	Lost to Seleucids
Seleucus IV 187–175 BC	Tried to plunder the temple	Ptolemy VI Philometer 181–146 BC	
Antiochus IV Epiphanes	Desecrated the temple in Jerusalem; provoked Maccabean revolt		

the Jews found themselves caught between the political struggles of the Ptolemies in Egypt and the Seleucids in Syria. Initially the Ptolemies took control of Judah and allowed the Jews to maintain their religious practices, although Greek customs became more common among the Jewish people, and they continued to speak Greek. It was during this period that the Greek translation of the Hebrew Bible, known as the Septuagint (LXX), was produced in Alexandria during the reign of Ptolemy Philadelphus (285–246 BC).

Hasmonean Rulers

John Hyrcanus I	134–104 BC	Last of the Maccabees
Aristobulus I	104–103 BC	Conquered Upper Galilee
Alexander Janneus	103–76 BC	Expanded Jewish Territory
Salome Alexandra	76–67 BC	Widow of Alexander
Hyrcanus II and Aristobulus II	67–63 BC	Rival sons of Salome Alexandra

Period of Independence

The reign of Antiochus IV was tumultuous; he attempted to force Hellenistic practices on the Jewish people. He even allowed two different men, Jason and Menelaus, to buy their way into the high priesthood for money. Eventually the Jews revolted against the Seleucids under the leadership of an aged priest named Matthias, who was from the village of Modein. Eventually his son Judas, nicknamed Maccabeus ("hammer"), led the revolt and captured Jerusalem. The temple was cleansed and rededicated on the 25th day of the month of Kislev in 167 BC according to the Hebrew calendar, which can fall at any point from late November to late December on the Gregorian calendar. This event is still commemorated today by the Jews as the Feast of Hanukkah (also known as the Festival of Lights).

Judas was later killed in battle in 166 BC. He was succeeded by his brother Jonathan, who gave his support to Alexander Balas in return for being appointed high priest in Jerusalem. In this way, both religious and civil rule were combined in one person. Jonathan was later killed in 143 BC. Another son of Matthias, Simon, ruled from 143–134 BC. Thereafter, the high priesthood was passed hereditarily to his descendants, who became what is known as the Hasmonean Dynasty.

In 134 BC, John Hyrcanus became both high priest and civil ruler, and remained so until 104 BC. During his administration he destroyed the Samaritan temple on Mount Gerizim and conquered the Idumeans of Edom. Alexander Janneus later became high priest and king during a long and violent reign (103–76 BC). His wife, Alexandria, ruled from 76–67 BC, while her son, Hyrcanus II, served as high priest. Later, a civil war between Hyrcanus II and his brother Aristobulus II ended with the Roman general Pompey taking control over the entire region.

When Pompey defeated Aristobulus, he named Antipater governor over Judea and Hyrcanus II as the high priest. Eventually Antipater's son Phasel was made governor of Judea, and his brother Herod was made governor of Galilee. Later, Antony and Octavian (Augustus Caesar) named Herod "King of the Jews" in 40 BC, and he ruled until his death in 4 BC. Herod, an Idumean by birth, married Mariamne, the granddaughter of Aristobulus II, whom he later had executed. A brilliant but brutal tyrant, Herod ruled with an iron fist over Judea, Samaria, Galilee, Perea, and Idumea. In an attempt to appease the Jews, Herod remodeled and expanded the Second Temple, making it one of the most glorious sanctuaries in the Roman World.

Jesus was born right at the end of Herod's rule circa 4 BC (following the current calendar). When the wise men (magi) arrived in Jerusalem looking for the baby who had been born "King of the Jews" (Matthew 2:2), Herod responded by ordering the execution of all male babies in the village of Bethlehem. Forewarned by an angel who appeared to Joseph in a dream, Jesus' family fled to Egypt. After Herod's death, Jesus' family returned from Egypt and settled in Nazareth in Galilee. In the meantime, Herod's kingdom was divided by his sons, with Antipas ruling Galilee and Perea, Philip in the Decapolis, and Archelaus in Judea and Samaria. After Archelaus was deposed in AD 6, Judea and Samaria were placed under Roman procurators who were under the governor of Syria. Thus, the stage was set for the New Testament era.

During the Intertestamental Period, the Jews produced many non-inspired writings. These included the books of the Apocrypha, many of which were included in the Latin Bible. Another group of some 50 books, known as the Pseudepigrapha, were never accepted in any collection of Scripture. In 1947, the Dead Sea Scrolls were discovered in caves at Qumran near the Dead Sea. These scrolls included copies or fragments from all the Old Testament books except Esther, as well as several nonbiblical works. These scrolls date from about 100 BC to AD 68.

Roman Rulers

66–63 BC	Pompey conquered Syria and Judea
60–53 BC	First Triumvirate: Julius Caesar, Pompey, and Crassus
49–45 BC	Civil War: Pompey vs. Julius Caesar
46 BC	Julius Caesar declared dictator of Rome
44 BC	Julius Caesar assassinated on March 15
42–31 BC	Conflicts between Antony and Octavian
31 BC	Octavian defeated Antony and Cleopatra
27 BC	Octavian given title "Augustus"
27 BC–AD 14	Augustus rules Imperial Rome; Jesus' birth
AD 14–37	Tiberius Caesar; Jesus' ministry

The Intertestamental Period
(Between OT and NT)

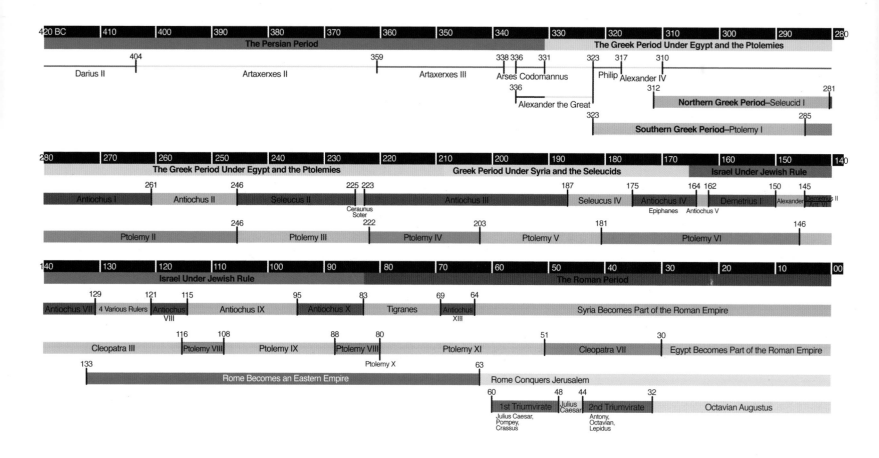

THE LIFE OF CHRIST

THE BIBLE MAKES BOLD CLAIMS about Jesus. It presents Him as the Son of God, the Savior of the world, and the Lord of the universe. The New Testament goes so far as to declare that our eternal destiny depends on our faith in Him (John 3:35-36).

From beginning to end, the Old Testament consistently predicted the coming of a Jewish Messiah. Jesus of Nazareth fulfilled more than 100 prophecies about His first coming: seed of the woman, son of Abraham, tribe of Judah, born of a virgin in Bethlehem, betrayed for 30 pieces of silver, pierced through His hands and feet, etc. That one individual fulfilled all these prophecies cannot be mere coincidence. Each one builds upon the others. Add them together, and you have convincing proof that Jesus was indeed the predicted Messiah.

Jesus claimed to have come from heaven, to be equal with God, to be the very incarnation of God, and to represent the power and authority of God. He was fully human, yet fully divine. Even His own disciples, who lived with Him during three years of ministry, were convinced that He was the Son of God (Matthew 14:33 16:16; John 1:49; 20:28).

Chronology of Jesus' Ministry

Jesus was born in Bethlehem circa 4 BC by the reckoning of our current calendar. At age 12 He visited the temple in Jerusalem with His earthly parents. Around AD 29, He began His public ministry, calling His first disciples (John 1:35-51). He attended the first Passover of His ministry on Nisan 14 (on the Jewish calendar), or April 7, AD 30 (John 2:13,23). After the Passover of AD 30, Jesus' ministry was primarily in Jerusalem and Judea (John 3:1-36). After the imprisonment of John the Baptist, Jesus passed through Samaria (John 4:4-42) and moved His focus to Galilee (John 4:43-46).

Between Passover of AD 31 and Passover of AD 32, Jesus' Galilean ministry reached its peak. It was at this time He preached the Sermon on the Mount (Matthew 5–7) and had an extensive healing ministry (Matthew 8–12). He appears to have returned to Jerusalem for the Feast of Tabernacles in the fall of AD 31 (John 5:1), and then withdrew again to Galilee (Luke 9:1-6). The miracle of the feeding of the 5000 came around Passover of AD 32 (John 6:1-15).

During the rest of AD 32, Jesus and the disciples withdrew to

Phoenicia (Matthew 15:21-28), and later went through the Decapolis to Caesarea-Philippi, where He announced that He would build His church (Matthew 16:13-20). It was during these months in Gentile territory that Jesus began to explain that His future church would contain both Jews and Gentiles.

Jesus later went to Jerusalem for the Feast of Tabernacles in the fall of AD 32 (John 7:2-10). He then returned to Galilee and later made His way back to Jerusalem for the Feast of Dedication (Hanukkah) in December AD 32, with an extensive ministry in Samaria and Perea en route (Luke 9:52-56; John 10:40-42). He later returned to Jerusalem again, and at this time raised Lazarus from the dead (John 11:1-18). Then He left for Ephraim, Samaria, and Galilee (John 11:54; Luke 17:11), from where He made His final journey with His disciples back to Jerusalem in the spring of AD 33.*

---

* See the detailed discussion of these dates and their related events in Harold Hoehner, *Chronological Aspects of the Life of Christ* (Grand Rapids, MI: Zondervan, 1977). See also A.J. Kostenberger and Justin Taylor, *The Final Days of Jesus* (Wheaton, IL: Crossway, 2014).

Jesus' Earthly Life

Birth at Bethlehem	c. 4 BC		Transfiguration	AD 32
Visit to temple at age 12	c. AD 8		Feast of Tabernacles	AD 32
Baptism by John the Baptist	AD 29		Later Judean ministry	AD 33
Calling the disciples	AD 29		Later Perean ministry	AD 33
Ministry in Samaria and Galilee	AD 30		Triumphal entry	AD 33
Great Galilean ministry	AD 31		Crucifixion	AD 33
Sermon on the Mount	AD 31		Resurrection	AD 33
Feeding of the 5000	AD 32		Ascension	AD 33
Travels to Phoenicia and Decapolis	AD 32			

The Life of Christ
(Gospels)

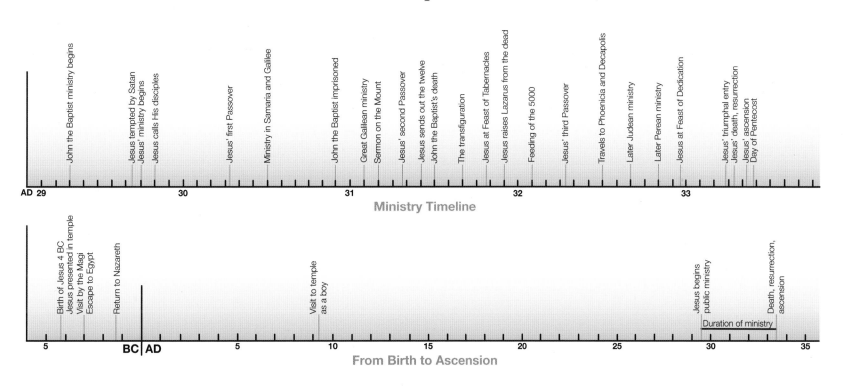

Ministry Timeline

John the Baptist ministry begins
Jesus tempted by Satan
Jesus' ministry begins
Jesus calls His disciples
Jesus' first Passover
Ministry in Samaria and Galilee
John the Baptist imprisoned
Great Galilean ministry
Sermon on the Mount
Jesus' second Passover
Jesus sends out the twelve
John the Baptist's death
The transfiguration
Jesus at Feast of Tabernacles
Jesus raises Lazarus from the dead
Feeding of the 5000
Jesus' third Passover
Travels to Phoenicia and Decapolis
Later Judean ministry
Later Perean ministry
Jesus at Feast of Dedication
Jesus' triumphal entry
Jesus' death, resurrection
Jesus' ascension
Day of Pentecost

AD 29   30   31   32   33

From Birth to Ascension

Birth of Jesus 4 BC
Jesus presented in temple
Visit by the Magi
Escape to Egypt
Return to Nazareth
Visit to temple as a boy
Jesus begins public ministry
Death, resurrection, ascension
Duration of ministry

5   BC | AD   5   10   15   20   25   30   35

30

TIMELINE OF MATTHEW 24–25

T HE OLIVET DISCOURSE is an important passage for the development of anyone's view of Bible prophecy. It is made up of our Lord's teaching on Bible prophecy, and it is found in Matthew 24–25, Mark 13, and Luke 21. Since one's interpretation of the Olivet Discourse greatly impacts whether he is a premillennialist or antimillennialist, futurist or preterist, or pretribulationist or posttribulationist, a proper understanding of Jesus' instruction is extremely important. It is also vital that one gets the chronology of these two chapters correct as well.

It's helpful to note the setting that leads up to Matthew's version of the Olivet Discourse. Christ had presented Himself to the Jewish people as their Messiah, but they rejected Him. Not only that, but their rulers led the way. Thus, like an Old Testament prophet, Jesus rebuked and exposed the nation's hypocrisy and unbelief in Matthew 22–23. Jesus noted that the present generation of Jewish leaders was like those of previous generations, who had killed the prophets before Him (23:29-36). Christ then told these leaders, "Truly I say to you, all these things will come upon this generation" (23:36). What things?

Jesus was referring to the curse of judgment, which came upon the Jewish people through the Roman army in AD 70.

As Matthew 24 opens, we see that Jesus is making His way from the temple (24:1) to the Mount of Olives (24:3). To do this, He would most likely have traveled down the Kidron Valley and then up to Olivet. As He was departing from the temple, "His disciples came up to point out the temple buildings to Him" (24:1). This statement leads us to believe that they were talking to Jesus about how beautiful the temple complex was, which Herod was still in the process of remodeling and refurbishing. The Lord must have startled His disciples as they gloated over the beauty of the temple complex when He said, "Do you not see all these things? Truly I say to you, not one stone here will be left upon another, which will not be torn down" (24:2). This is Christ's only reference to the destruction of the temple in all of Matthew 24–25.

After Christ's statement there is a break in the narrative, which picks up in verse 3, saying, "As He was sitting on the Mount of Olives, the disciples came to Him privately." The disciples then asked, "Tell us, when will these things be, and what will be the sign of Your coming, and of the end of the age?" (24:3). Their first question relates to the destruction of the temple, yet Christ's answer is not reported in Matthew, but in Luke 21. Matthew only gives our Lord's reply to "what will be the sign of Your coming, and the end of the age?" (24:3).

Jesus' discourse begins in 24:4, where He speaks of the events of the first half of the seven-year Tribulation in verses 4-14. These are called "the beginning of birth pangs" and involve false christs, wars, rumors of wars, famines, pestilence, persecution, and earthquakes (24:4-13). The judgments described in Matthew 24:4-13 parallel, in order, the first six seal judgments of Revelation 6:1-11, which will also occur during the first half of the Tribulation. During this same time, the gospel of the kingdom will be preached in the whole world (Matthew 24:14).

The midpoint of the Tribulation is described next (24:15-20). Jesus spoke of the abomination of desolation, when the Antichrist desecrates the holy place in the rebuilt Jewish temple in Jerusalem. This is to be a sign to Jewish believers that they should flee into the wilderness for safety (24:16-20). We know from Old Testament passages that the Jewish remnant will escape to Petra in southern Jordan and will be protected there by the Lord.

The second half of the Tribulation, called the Great Tribulation (24:21), will then begin to unfold (24:21-26). This will be a time during which no life would survive if the Lord were not to intervene (24:22). It will be a time during which false Christs and false prophets will abound and show great signs and wonders for the purpose of deceiving people, but their destiny will be one of judgment (24:24-26).

At the end of the seven-year Tribulation, Jesus the Messiah will return to earth, specifically to Jerusalem and the Mount of Olives, to rescue all believers, especially Jewish believers (24:27-31). During the second coming, angels will be sent to gather up all the Jewish believers from around the world in order to bring them to Jerusalem in preparation for the start of the 1000-year reign of Christ over the earth (24:31).

At the end of chapter 24, Christ taught a series of parables (24:32-51). In the parable of the fig tree (24:32-35), He addressed the disciples' question about the signs leading up to His second coming. Jesus said that the generation that saw all of the signs described in verses 4-26 would also see His return (24:27-31). Since the time period of the Tribulation is seven years, then it does not matter how long a generation is since the period of signs is only a seven-year period.

The fig tree parable does not relate to the modern reestablishment of the nation of Israel; there are other passages related to Israel's becoming a modern nation. Some Bible interpreters believe that the fig tree is a symbol for Israel and the generation (usually viewed as a 40-year period) that sees the reestablishment of Israel as a nation, which will also see Christ's second coming within 40 years. Since Israel was founded in 1948, it would mean that Christ's return should have occurred by 1988, which did not happen. There are a couple key problems with that view: First, the statement by Christ about the generation that sees all these things is not a prophecy; instead, it is an illustration that when the signs of the Tribulation begin to occur, Christ's coming is near. Second, Matthew 24:4-31 only covers the events of the seven-year Tribulation and not a 40-year period; thus, the generation that sees these signs begin to occur will go through a seven-year period until the coming of Christ. That said, there are other passages related to Israel's becoming a modern nation (Ezekiel 20:33-38; 22:17-22; 36:22-24; 38–39; Isaiah 11:11-12; Zephaniah 2:1-2).

The rest of the parables are given to the nation of Israel and speak about watchfulness and readiness in the light of the Tribulation events the Lord mentioned in His discourse (24:36-51). While the nation of Israel rejected Jesus as their Messiah at His first coming, they can be ready for Him at His second coming.

Chapter 25 begins with two more parables for the nation of Israel (25:1-30). The parable of the ten virgins does not relate to the church or the rapture. Rather, this parable speaks of some Jewish people who are prepared for the coming of Messiah. Their preparation is evident by the fact they had oil in their lamps, in anticipation of the arrival of the Bridegroom, who will come unexpectedly in the middle of the night (25:1-13). The parable about the talents deals with whether a Jewish person will be faithful during the interim. Jesus spoke of a landlord who went on a long journey (25:14-30). The one who is faithful

Timeline of Matthew 24–25

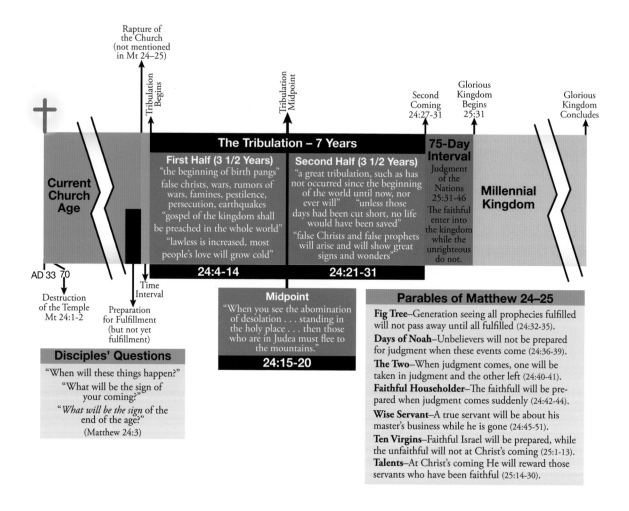

Rapture of
the Church
(not mentioned
in Mt 24–25)

Tribulation
Begins

Tribulation
Midpoint

Second
Coming
24:27-31

Glorious
Kingdom
Begins
25:31

Glorious
Kingdom
Concludes

The Tribulation – 7 Years

**Current
Church
Age**

First Half (3 1/2 Years)
"the beginning of birth pangs"
false christs, wars, rumors of
wars, famines, pestilence,
persecution, earthquakes
"gospel of the kingdom shall
be preached in the whole world"
"lawless is increased, most
people's love will grow cold"

24:4-14

Second Half (3 1/2 Years)
"a great tribulation, such as has
not occurred since the beginning
of the world until now, nor
ever will" "unless those
days had been cut short, no life
would have been saved"
"false Christs and false prophets
will arise and will show great
signs and wonders"

24:21-31

**75-Day
Interval**
Judgment
of the
Nations
25:31-46
The faithful
enter into
the kingdom
while the
unrighteous
do not.

**Millennial
Kingdom**

AD 33 70

Destruction
of the Temple
Mt 24:1-2

Time
Interval

Preparation
for Fulfillment
(but not yet
fulfillment)

Midpoint
"When you see the abomination
of desolation . . . standing in
the holy place . . . then those
who are in Judea must flee to
the mountains."

24:15-20

Disciples' Questions

"When will these things happen?"
"What will be the sign of
your coming?"
"*What will be the sign* of the
end of the age?"
(Matthew 24:3)

Parables of Matthew 24–25

Fig Tree–Generation seeing all prophecies fulfilled
will not pass away until all fulfilled (24:32-35).

Days of Noah–Unbelievers will not be prepared
for judgment when these events come (24:36-39).

The Two–When judgment comes, one will be
taken in judgment and the other left (24:40-41).

Faithful Householder–The faithfull will be prepared when judgment comes suddenly (24:42-44).

Wise Servant–A true servant will be about his
master's business while he is gone (24:45-51).

Ten Virgins–Faithful Israel will be prepared, while
the unfaithful will not at Christ's coming (25:1-13).

Talents–At Christ's coming He will reward those
servants who have been faithful (25:14-30).

---

in the absence of his boss will be rewarded with greater responsibility when the boss returns. That's what will happen when Messiah returns to set up His kingdom.

The final section of chapter 25—verses 31 to 46—speaks of the judgment of Gentiles: "When the Son of Man comes in His glory, and all the angels with Him, then He will sit on His glorious throne"

(25:31). This judgment will determine who is saved and who is lost. Lost Gentiles—that is, the goats in this parable—will not be permitted entry into the glorious kingdom of the Messiah. Saved Gentiles, however, will be welcomed into the Messiah's kingdom. They bore the fruit that would be evident in the life of a saved individual by risking their lives to help save persecuted Jews during the Tribulation.

31

CHRONOLOGY OF THE NEW TESTAMENT CHURCH

THE BOOK OF ACTS PROVIDES the only Holy Spirit-inspired account of the birth and growth of the early church. The human author of Acts was Luke, who began by sharing the details of the birth of the church in AD 33 on the Day of Pentecost (Acts 2). Some see Acts as the New Testament parallel to the Old Testament book of Joshua, which documents Israel's entrance into the Promised Land and its spreading occupation of that land. Acts 1:8 provides an outline of the book as the early church is established in Jerusalem, then spreads to Judea and Samaria, then globally to the remotest parts of the earth. In Acts 1:8 appears the Great Commission, the marching orders for the newly founded church, and they are still our Lord's desire for the church today, 2000 years later.

Luke's purpose for writing Acts was to provide God's viewpoint for the founding of the new organism known as the body of Christ, or the church. In Acts, Luke also provides a defense of Christianity. Acts is seen as Luke's second and last volume in his series on the words and works of Christ, with the Gospel of Luke being volume one.

The chronology of the book of Acts is the chronology of the founding and development of the early church. Acts 1 speaks of the preparation for the church's birth, during which time the resurrected Christ spent 40 days teaching truths concerning the kingdom of God (Acts 1:3). The church was never spoken of in the Old Testament; though it was always a part of God's master plan, it was kept hidden as a mystery until revealed through the apostle Paul (Romans 16:25-26; Ephesians 3:1-10; Colossians 1:26-27).

Fifty days after the death of Christ—on the Day of Pentecost—the church was born (Acts 2). Initially it was made up of Jews from Jerusalem and throughout Israel. Acts chapters 3 through 8 tell of the expansion of the church among the Jews of Jerusalem, as well as the persecution they faced from the leaders of Judaism. When Stephen, the first martyr of the church, was stoned to death (Acts 8), the scene was set for the conversion of Saul, who was one of the most zealous persecutors of the people in the early church.

As the church moved beyond Jerusalem to other parts of Israel, Saul was converted on the road to Damascus. Christ set him apart to spread the gospel beyond Israel into the Gentile world. Saul, also

Chronology of the New Testament Church
(Acts)

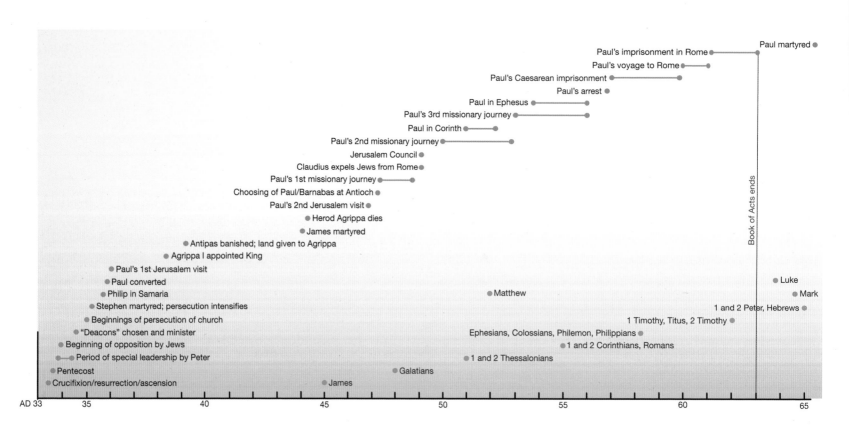

Paul martyred ●

Paul's imprisonment in Rome ●————●

Paul's voyage to Rome ●——●

Paul's Caesarean imprisonment ●————————●

Paul's arrest ●

Paul in Ephesus ●——————●

Paul's 3rd missionary journey ●————————●

Paul in Corinth ●————●

Paul's 2nd missionary journey ●——————————●

Jerusalem Council ●

Claudius expels Jews from Rome ●

Paul's 1st missionary journey ●————●

Choosing of Paul/Barnabas at Antioch ●

Paul's 2nd Jerusalem visit ●

● Herod Agrippa dies

● James martyred

● Antipas banished; land given to Agrippa

● Agrippa I appointed King

● Paul's 1st Jerusalem visit

● Paul converted

● Philip in Samaria

● Stephen martyred; persecution intensifies

● Beginnings of persecution of church

● "Deacons" chosen and minister

● Beginning of opposition by Jews

●——● Period of special leadership by Peter

● Pentecost

●——● Crucifixion/resurrection/ascension

● Matthew

● Luke

● Mark

1 and 2 Peter, Hebrews ●

1 Timothy, Titus, 2 Timothy ●

Ephesians, Colossians, Philemon, Philippians ●

● 1 and 2 Corinthians, Romans

● 1 and 2 Thessalonians

● Galatians

● James

Book of Acts ends

AD 33   35   40   45   50   55   60   65

known as Paul, was chosen to become the apostle to the Gentiles. After a number of years of preparation, Paul began spreading the gospel throughout Israel and into Syria, a Gentile land in which he was raised. As Gentiles were added to the body of Christ, there were a number of reactions within the land of Israel. In addition to physical persecution from King Herod, there also arose doctrinal division. The Jerusalem church, made up almost entirely of Jewish believers, sponsored a council that concluded that Gentiles do not have to first convert to Judaism in order to put themselves into a position where they could then believe in Christ for salvation. Instead, the council decreed that anyone, including Gentiles, may simply believe in Christ to be saved from their sins (Acts 15).

Paul's first missionary journey is described in Acts 13–14, and it was the shortest of the three journeys. Paul took the gospel to Antioch (his hometown), Cyprus, and to various cities in Galatia. His second missionary journey is recorded in Acts 15–18. He began that journey by revisiting churches he went to on his previous trip. In chapter 16, as Paul headed east, he received the famous Macedonian vision and immediately headed west into Europe. During this trip Paul established many new churches throughout Macedonia and Greece, with visits to Thessalonica, Berea, Athens, and Corinth. Acts recorded Paul's travels as real historical events, which they were. The accounts were not given merely to teach spiritual principles, but to relate real historical events that actually happened. We can visit these same locations today and follow in the footsteps of the apostle's first-century journeys.

The third missionary journey is described in Acts 18:23–21:26. During that trip, Paul visited Greece and Asia Minor, or what is now western Turkey.

After his third missionary journey, Paul returned to Jerusalem and was arrested by the Jewish religious leaders. Because he was a Roman citizen, he was able to make an appeal for his case to be heard before Caesar. This, in turn, meant Paul was able to take the gospel to Rome. But before he was sent, he was brought before the Roman rulers in Israel, making his famous defenses before Felix (Acts 24), Festus (Acts 25), and Agrippa (Acts 26). Then during the journey to Rome, he was shipwrecked and landed on the island of Malta (Acts 27). In Acts 28, we see Paul in Rome, under house arrest and awaiting his trial. All through this time, he continued to spread the gospel message.

The book of Acts closes with what some consider to be an incomplete sentence. But the intent here was to show that the work of preaching the gospel to the ends of the earth is still moving forward, even though the accounts of what happened in the early church have come to an end, the spread of the gospel is ongoing.

NEW TESTAMENT LETTERS

THE LETTERS OF THE APOSTLES, also known as epistles, deal with personal, practical, and theological matters. The earliest letters reflect the discussions within the early church over the relationship of the Old Testament Law to New Testament grace. The earliest letters were written around AD 45–50, and the latter ones as late as AD 90–95. Thirteen letters were by the apostle Paul (and possibly Hebrews), two by Peter, three by John, one by James, and one by Jude.

The chronological arrangement of the apostolic letters has been greatly debated and is being continually examined. Following the traditional dates for these letters, we have suggested the following arrangement.

James is traditionally ascribed to James, the brother of Jesus, pastor of the Jerusalem church and moderator of the Jerusalem Council. It was addressed to the "twelve tribes who are dispersed abroad" and was probably written between AD 45–50. James emphasized the nature of true religion by declaring its spiritual dimensions and practical application.

Galatians was written by the apostle Paul to the churches of Galatia in Asia Minor. He ministered there during his three missionary journeys (Acts 14:21-23). The letter itself was written in the form of a protest against corrupting the gospel of salvation by grace alone. Paul condemned, in no uncertain terms, the idea of salvation by works. While the dating of the letter is debated, most believe it was written in AD 48, which is around or just after the time of the Jerusalem Council.

First and 2 Thessalonians were written a few months apart in AD 51 during Paul's stay at Corinth. Both letters deal with matters related to the second coming of Christ. The first letter explains the rapture of believers (1 Thessalonians 4:13-17), and the second letter explains details regarding the removal of "the restrainer" (the Holy Spirit), the revealing of the Antichrist, and the ultimate return of Christ. That these topics were of such importance indicates they were essential doctrines in the early church.

First and 2 Corinthians were written from Ephesus. The first letter was carried by Timothy and employs a wide range of literary styles: exposition, narration, logic, sarcasm, and poetry. It includes a response to strife and conflict in the church as well as Paul's answers to various questions regarding marriage, things sacrificed to idols, issues of worship, and spiritual gifts. It also includes his extensive exposition on the resurrection of the body. The second letter is highly personal, with Paul giving an extensive defense of his ministry.

Romans was written from Corinth and sent to Rome by Phoebe, a deaconess of the church in Cenchrea (16:1). Paul mentioned numerous acquaintances at Rome but had not yet visited them there when this letter was written. Romans is the most doctrinal of all of Paul's letters, emphasizing the depravity of man, the sovereignty of God, the righteousness of Christ, the nature of salvation by faith, God's promises to Israel, and matters relating to personal, practical, public, and political issues.

The four *prison epistles* (Ephesians, Philippians, Colossians, and Philemon) were written between AD 56–60, most likely from Rome. All of them make references to Paul's "bonds," and Philippians 4:22 specifically refers to "Caesar's household" and to the praetorian guard (1:13), which seems more applicable to Rome than Caesarea, where Paul had been imprisoned earlier.

Ephesians was probably meant to be a circular, or a letter circulated among and read by the churches of Asia Minor, which Paul had visited before his imprisonment. The messenger of this letter was Tychicus, whom Onesimus accompanied (Ephesians 6:21; Colossians 4:7-9). The Ephesian letter emphasizes God's plan of redemption, the ministry of the Holy Spirit, and the practical walk of the Christian believer.

Colossians was also written to believers in Asia Minor, whom Paul had not visited (2:1). Much of his letter to them emphasized Paul's Christology. He pictured Christ as pre-eminent in creation in general and in the life of the church in particular. In Him, all the fullness of deity resides (1:19) and in Him are hidden all the treasures of wisdom and knowledge (2:3).

Philemon is a personal letter written at the same general time as Ephesians and Colossians. Philemon was a Christian believer and businessman from Colosse. In the letter, Paul urged Philemon to forgive and receive his runaway slave Onesimus, who had been converted to Christ by Paul's witness. This brief letter is an excellent example of the practical implications of the gospel. Paul asked Philemon to receive Onesimus not as a slave, but as "a beloved brother" (verse 16).

Philippians was written to the church in Philippi in Macedonia, where Paul first ministered a decade earlier. The church sent Epaphroditus to Rome with gifts for Paul, and he, in turn, sent him back with this letter (2:28-29). Philippians emphasizes the power of the gospel (1:12,16,27) and the joy of the Christian life (1:4; 2:1,16,18,28; 3:1; 4:4). In this very personal letter, Paul made the declaration, "For to me, to live is Christ and to die is gain" (1:21).

The *pastoral epistles* appear to have been written around the time of the prison epistles (on the basis of their references to Paul's companions). The personal and biographical data that can be gleaned from Paul's letters and the book of Acts seem to indicate that he was acquitted and released in AD 60–61. Evidently he was able to travel again for a brief time, during which he probably wrote 1 Timothy and Titus. However, the tone of 2 Timothy clearly indicates Paul was back in prison, for he said, "The time of my departure [death] has come" (4:6-7).

First Timothy addressed the growing organizational development of the early churches. Bishops, deacons, and elders were defined and their duties described. Church services, following the pattern of the Jewish synagogues, included reading, preaching, praying, and laying on of hands. Paul had sent Timothy back to Ephesus and was now charging him with the responsibility of carrying on the ministry there. Timothy had been with Paul during his first imprisonment (Colossians 1:1) and later rejoined him at Rome (2 Timothy 4:11,21).

Titus was a Gentile convert from Paul's first missionary journey (Galatians 2:1-3). He also travelled with Paul on his third missionary journey (see 2 Corinthians 7:6-16). While Titus was overseeing a church on the island of Crete, Paul wrote this letter, which contains the strongest creedal formulation of the church's theology, including the deity of Christ (2:13), the ministry of the Holy Spirit (3:5), salvation by grace (3:5), justification by faith (3:7), and the "blessed hope" of Christ's return (2:13).

Second Timothy clearly identifies Paul as being back in prison (1:8). Many believe he was arrested suddenly, possibly at Troas, and taken

New Testament Epistles

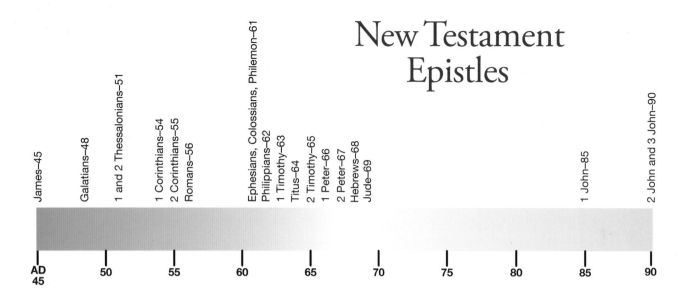

back to Rome, leaving his cloak and scrolls behind (4:13).[1] This was his last letter before his eventual execution by Nero in Rome. In this letter, Paul passed on his legacy to Timothy, emphasizing that "I have fought the good fight, I have finished the course, I have kept the faith" (4:7).

Hebrews was written to Jewish Christians in general to clarify the superiority of the Christian faith. The letter was apparently written to second-generation believers (2:1-4) long after their conversion (10:32; 13:7). Timothy had been imprisoned but was still alive (13:23), and references to the priesthood indicate the temple was still standing at the time. Thus, a date of circa AD 68 is most likely. The letter has often been ascribed to Paul, but unlike all his other letters, it is unsigned.

First and 2 Peter were written during the late mid-first century, around AD 66–68. The first letter was addressed to "pilgrims of the Dispersion" (1:1 NKJV) who were facing persecution for their faith. Filled with more than 30 imperatives (for example, be sober, be holy, love, fear, etc.), the letter's directions resemble messages Peter preached. The second letter was written to combat false teaching and to remind believers of the promise of Christ's sudden return "as a thief in the night" (3:10).

Jude was written by the brother of James, also the half brother of Jesus. The fact that verses 17-18 quote verbatim from 2 Peter 3:3 indicates Jude was familiar with Peter's letter. This would seem to indicate he was writing sometime between AD 68–70. The main focus of his letter was to urge the believers to "contend earnestly for the faith" (verse 3). In the spirit of grace, Jude urged mercy in rescuing heretics from the pit of unbelief (verses 21-23).

First, 2, and 3 John were letters written by the author of John's Gospel. Many suggest the second and third letters may have been written as introductory notes of private counsel and greeting to accompany the main body of teaching expressed in the first letter.[2] Much of the main letter was written to combat the growing heresy of Gnosticism at the end of the first century (this heresy denied the deity and humanity of Christ). For this reason, most date these letters between AD 90–95.

These latter letters of the New Testament provide a solid front against the rising tide of heresies in the mid to late first century. All of them draw a clear distinction between truth and error, light and darkness, and life and death. Merrill Tenney noted, "They presuppose a clear and perfected revelation of eternal life in Christ which constitutes the standard of truth which must be accepted or rejected by men."[3]

BOOK OF REVELATION TIMELINE

THE BOOK OF REVELATION is the capstone of the 66 books of the Bible and is a fitting conclusion to the biblical canon. Within Revelation is a verse that provides its own outline for the book: "Write the things which you have seen, and the things which are, and the things which will take place after these things" (Revelation 1:19). This threefold division becomes evident as one reads through Revelation: Chapter 1 speaks of the "the things which you have seen," which includes the glorified Christ. Chapters 2 and 3 correspond with "the things which are," as the letters to the seven churches have to do with the present church age. And the rest of the book (chapters 4–22) reveals "the things which will take place after these things." Everything from chapter 4 onward speaks of times and events future to our own day. These future eras refer to the Tribulation (4–19), the Millennium (20), and the eternal state (21–22).

Revelation is filled with Old Testament allusions. While the Old Testament is not directly quoted a single time, there are at least 550 allusions to it.[1] The apostle John was told to write what he saw in the visions (1:11,19). As he did so, under the inspiration of the Holy Spirit, he used words and phrases from the Old Testament prophets that result in Revelation linking many of these Old Testament passages to a general timeline in the last book of the Bible. As a result, a general chronology is set forth of (1) the current church age; (2) the rapture implied in 4:1; (3) a detailed account of events of the Tribulation, (4); Christ's second coming; (5) the millennial kingdom; (6) the Great White Throne Judgment; and (7) the eternal state, which goes on forever.

Let's take a closer look now at the threefold division of the book:

The things which you have seen—This speaks of the glorified Christ, who is described in chapter 1. Jesus' persona was nothing like John had ever seen before during our Lord's ministry on earth. Jesus was proclaiming that He was going to be a judge.

The things which are—This presents Jesus as doing a careful inspection of the seven churches of Asia. These evaluations refer to real first-century churches and reveal their positives and negatives. They also represent churches all through the church age, up to today.

The things which will take place after these things—Immediately

Revelation Timeline

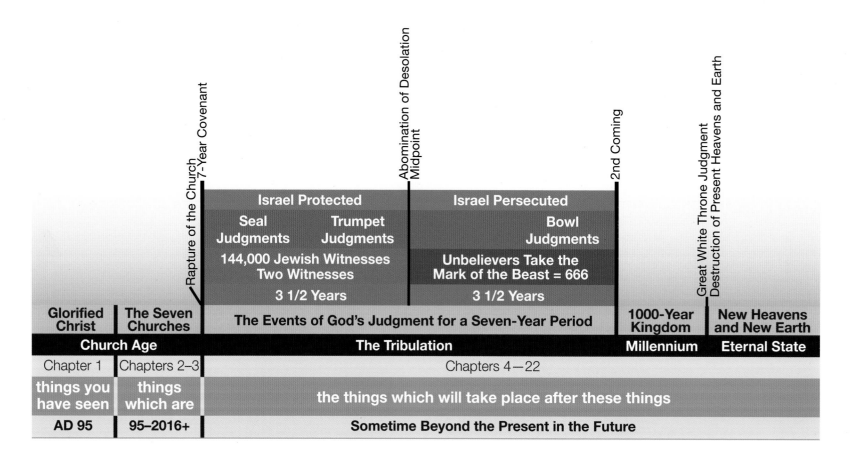

"Therefore write the things which you have seen, the things which are,
and the things which will take place after these things" (Revelation 1:19).

after the seventh church was described and just before God's judgments were poured out, John, a member of the church, was taken up into heaven (Revelation 4:1-2). This passage demonstrates the church's position in relation to the wrath that will come upon the earth during the Tribulation. That is, the church will be taken up to heaven prior to the Tribulation. This is affirmed by specific passages in the New Testament epistles—passages that support the pretribulation rapture view.

The chronology of the Tribulation, as given in the book of Revelation, is generally sequential; however, there are places where we find pauses in the chronological unfolding of events so that information can be presented topically. Chapters 4 and 5 introduce the events of the Tribulation as ultimately emanating from the throne of God the Father and the Lamb. Chapter 6 speaks of the beginning of the Tribulation, during which six seal judgments are poured out as God expresses His wrath upon the people of the earth (6:16-17). Chapter 7 introduces 144,000 male Jewish witnesses (7:1-8) whom God will use to introduce salvation in Christ to "a great multitude which no one could count" (7:9-17). Chapters 8 and 9 describe the six trumpet judgments, which will take place before the midpoint of the seven years.

Chapters 10–15 all deal with topical issues at the midpoint of the seven years. Chapter 11 presents the ministry of the two witnesses, which takes place during the first half of the Tribulation. Chapter 12 tells about the woman (Israel) who flees into the wilderness and is miraculously protected by the Lord during the second half of the Tribulation. Chapter 13 speaks of two beasts—the first beast is the Antichrist (13:1-10), and the second is the false prophet (13:11-18). Chapter 14 includes the three angelic announcements (14:6-13). Chapter 16 describes the seven bowl judgments that will be poured out during the second half of the Tribulation. Chapters 17 and 18 speak of a revived city of Babylon and its influence in three major spheres: religious, civil, and economic.

In chapter 19 the Tribulation is coming to an end with the glorious second advent of the Lord Jesus Christ (19:11-21). Chapter 20 speaks of the binding of Satan for 1000 years and the kingdom reign of Christ with the saints for 1000 years (20:4-6). At the end of the Millennium, Satan will be released and make one last stand. But God will destroy him quickly, as well as his human followers (20:7-10). Then will come the Great White Throne Judgment, at which time human history will end (20:11-15).

The last section of Revelation describes the eternal state (21–22). The present heavens and earth will be destroyed and replaced by a new heavens and earth (21:1). This new world will contain the New Jerusalem, which is said to be 1500 miles square and high, and John describes an amazing eternity for all believers throughout history (21:2–22:5). Revelation closes with a final appeal to the unbeliever: "The Spirit and the bride say, 'Come.' And let the one who hears say, 'Come.' And let the one who is thirsty come; let the one who wishes take the water of life without cost" (22:17).

34

FUTURE EVENTS

THE BIBLE DEMONSTRATES its supernatural origin in that it not only records past events accurately, but it also speaks of future events with just as much veracity. The extent to which Scripture speaks concerning the future allows one to map out a chronology of coming events in some detail. That chronology of future events is the focus of this chapter.

The church age has continued for almost 2000 years now. We are likely toward the end of this time period, because God appears to be setting the stage for events that the Bible says will take place after the rapture, or during the Tribulation. The people of Israel are back in their homeland, primarily in unbelief. Globalism has become more and more a way of everyday life. The European Union appears to be a forerunner of the revived Roman Empire. The Gog and Magog invasion appears imminent as Russia and Iran are working together for the first time in history.

The rapture of the church, which will suddenly bring the church age to an end, is the next prophesied event on the biblical calendar, and it could happen at any moment. There are no signs that one will be able to observe that will indicate the rapture is about to take place. That is why the church, the bride of Christ, is to constantly be ready for the possibility that Christ may come at any moment. After the rapture occurs, the man of lawlessness—or the Antichrist—will be allowed by the Holy Spirit to begin putting himself into place for what is to come during the Tribulation.

After the rapture but before the start of the Tribulation is when we will most likely see the invasion of Israel as prophesied in Ezekiel 38–39. The Gog and Magog invasion will result in a supernatural intervention by the Lord on behalf of His regathered people, and the total destruction of the invaders and the lands from which they came. Most of the nations in this coalition will be comprised of non-Arab Muslims led by Russia, and this event will probably greatly reduce the Islamic threat that is on the rise all across the globe today.

The next event will be the 70th week of Daniel (Daniel 9:27), which is also known as the seven-year Tribulation. This time is also called the "covenant with death" in relation to Israel (Isaiah 28:15,18). In Jeremiah 30:7, it is called the "the time of Jacob's distress." Jeremiah goes on to say that Israel will be delivered from it. Daniel 12:1 says, "There will be a time of distress [tribulation] such as never occurred since there was a nation until that time." Jesus quotes this passage in Matthew 24:21. The purpose of the Tribulation for Israel, then, is to purge out unbelieving Israel so that only believing Israel is left by the end of the Tribulation (Ezekiel 20:33-44; Daniel 12:10; Zechariah 13:8-9). For the Gentiles, the Tribulation is a time of God's wrath and testing (Isaiah 24:1-20; 26:21; Revelation 3:10).

At the midpoint of the seven-year period will occur the "abomination of desolation," which is first mentioned in Daniel 9:27. Jesus also spoke of it in Matthew 24:15 and admonished the reader to understand what Daniel was speaking about. The abomination of desolation refers to an event that defiles Israel's rebuilt temple. This is likely what Paul was referring to in 2 Thessalonians 2:4 when he said that the man of lawlessness (or the Antichrist) would take "his seat in the temple of God, displaying himself as being God." In Matthew 24, Jesus advised the Jews to escape into the wilderness when they saw this abomination taking place.

The Campaign of Armageddon will take place in eight stages (see chapter 35 for more details). This series of events will lead up to the second coming of Christ. The Antichrist and false prophet will bring the armies of the world into northern Israel in preparation for an attack on Jerusalem, God's city. However, Christ Himself will descend from heaven—in the second coming—to destroy Antichrist's army and rescue Israel.

In Acts 1, when Jesus ascended to heaven, the disciples were told that He would return in exactly the same manner in which He was ascending. At this point it's important to observe that the rapture is not the same event as the second coming. At the rapture, Christ will not return all the way to planet Earth. Instead, He will hover in the clouds, and those who are genuinely saved will be taken up into the clouds to meet Him in the air. Then Jesus and all the raptured believers will return to the Father's house in heaven.

By contrast, at the second coming, Christ will come all the way down to planet Earth at the Mount of Olives in Jerusalem in order to rescue believing Israel and believing Gentiles. Then He will set up His 1000-year kingdom on earth.

Revelation 19:11-16 presents Christ as He has never before appeared in history. He is in battle dress for the purpose of judging His enemies, who have been proven all through history to be unjust rebels against the Triune God. Christ will return riding a white horse with the intent to judge, as depicted by His flaming eyes and clothes dipped in blood (19:12-13). He will destroy His enemies with a mere word (Revelation 19:12,15). With a word He spoke creation into existence (Genesis 1–2), and with a word He will bring judgment and destruction. Christ's bride will follow closely behind Him on white horses (Revelation 19:14). Judgment must precede the establishment of His millennial kingdom (described in Revelation 20). Evil cannot be allowed to exist in a righteous kingdom.

Daniel 12 indicates that there will be a 75-day interval between the day of Christ's second coming and the start of the millennial kingdom. During this interval, the Messiah will bring with Him, from heaven, a new temple that is one mile square (Ezekiel 40). It is at this new temple that the sacrificial system will return during the Millennium. Also, during this same 75-day interval, the sheep and goat judgment will take place so that no unbeliever will enter into Christ's righteous kingdom. After the 75-day period ends, Christ will reign from Jerusalem for 1000 years.

In a sense, Revelation 20:7-10 describes the "second coming of Satan." Instead of coming from the Father's right hand, as will our Lord Jesus Christ, Satan will be released from his prison in the bowels of the earth (20:7). At the end of his 1000-year term, he is just as evil as he has ever been. And the same will be true about mankind.

Why will Satan be released from the abyss? He "will come out to deceive the nations which are in the four corners of the earth…to gather them together for the war" (20:8). We are told the "number of them is like the sand of the seashore," and that they will come up to "the broad plain of the earth and surround the camp of the saints and the beloved city" (20:9), which is Jerusalem.

Some have said those who participate in this rebellion would have to be utterly stupid to try to come up against a city that is inhabited by a mixture of resurrected and mortal humans, not to mention God Himself. However crazy it may be, it is yet another monumental demonstration of the foolishness to which sin and rebellion against God drives individuals.

We consider it an even greater folly for Satan to have fallen into sin at the beginning of history, for he was surrounded by the presence of the Triune God and His entire court in the heavenly throne room. In Revelation 20, God will use Satan's rebellion like a magnet to draw to Satan all those who, like him, have unregenerate hearts. Before this uprising, with Christ on His throne ruling with a rod of iron, the unregenerate will not have the corporate courage to revolt against the Lord. They will want to rebel, but only with the assistance of a bold leader—Satan.

How will God deal with this final revolt? He will not take another seven years to put it down, as He did during the Tribulation. Instead, He will dispense of it in a moment by calling fire to come "down from heaven and devour them" (20:9). Satan will become the third person to be cast into the Lake of Fire, his eternal abode, preceded by his two cohorts in crime, the Antichrist and false prophet (20:10). The text tells us, "They will be tormented day and night forever and ever" (20:10). This is one of the many clear statements in Scripture that teach that punishment in the Lake of Fire is eternal and will never come to an end.

After Satan is taken care of, John next sees "a great white throne and Him who sat upon it, from whose presence earth and heaven fled away, and no place was found for them" (20:11). This is the final judgment for all unbelievers, and *only* unbelievers. John looks again and sees "the dead, the great and the small, standing before the throne" (20:12). Every individual who has rejected the free offer of the gospel of Christ will now have to literally stand before God themselves

Future Events

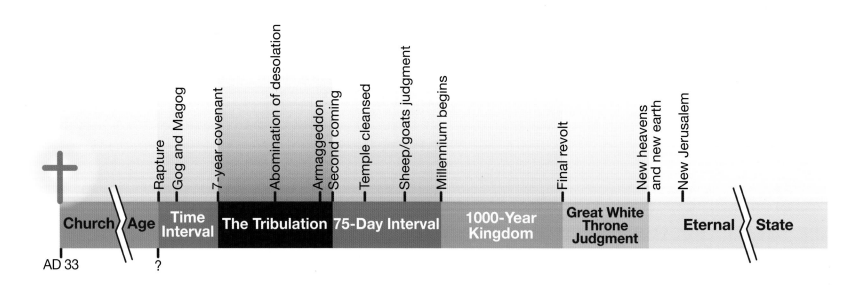

to give an account for their sins. Every unbeliever down through history will have to do this.

On what basis will all the unbelievers of the ages be judged? They will be judged "according to their deeds" (20:12). By what standard will their deeds be measured against? This judgment will not be an evaluation of how a person compares to fellow human beings. Rather, everyone will be compared to God's righteous character and the demands that He has made regarding holiness. Scripture teaches that "all our righteous deeds are like a filthy garment" (Isaiah 64:6). If that is the value before God of the *best* that anyone has to offer, can you imagine what God thinks of our evil deeds? There is no hope for anyone to pass God's judgment, apart from Christ. But these people have all rejected Christ; that's why they are standing before the Great White Throne. And what will their destiny be? The Bible says they will be "thrown into the lake of fire" (20:15) to join the three who are already there.

Next, John turns our attention to eternity and introduces us to "a new heaven and a new earth; for the first heaven and the first earth passed away" (21:1). Peter also spoke concerning the new heavens and new earth when he said that the present universe "will pass away with a roar and the elements will be destroyed with intense heat, and the earth and its works will be burned up" (2 Peter 3:10). He further describes the passing of our present world when he adds that "the heavens will be destroyed by burning, and the elements will melt with intense heat" (3:12). Then God will replace our present universe with "new heavens and a new earth, in which righteousness dwells" (3:13).

John then closes by describing the New Jerusalem (21:2–22:5). Of all the great cities in the history of the world, only Jerusalem will have an eternal continuance. The New Jerusalem, which will have already been built in heaven, will come down "out of heaven from God, made ready as a bride adorned for her husband" (21:2). This place will be the most amazing city ever. Prior to the New Jerusalem, all other cities will have been built by man. With the advent of the New Jerusalem, God will show all creation how a city ought to be built. With the arrival of this celestial city, history will have progressed from an undeveloped garden to a divinely built city. Now that's progress!

What a great and glorious future all believers in Christ have awaiting them in eternity. And even with all that we know about eternity from Revelation 21–22, the apostle Paul reminds us that we know only a tiny fraction of what God has in store for believers—"things which eye has not seen and ear has not heard, And which have not entered the heart of man, all that God has prepared for those who love Him" (1 Corinthians 2:9).

35

THE TRIBULATION TIMELINE

THE SEVEN-YEAR TRIBULATION is mentioned throughout Scripture numerous times, in both the Old and New Testaments. It is referred to as "the day of the LORD" or "the great day of the LORD" (Joel 2:1,11; 3:14; Zephaniah 1:7,14,18; 2:3), the "tribulation" or "great tribulation" (Matthew 24:9,21,29; Revelation 7:14), time of God's "wrath" (Zephaniah 1:15; 1 Thessalonians 1:10; 5:9; Revelation 6:16-17; 11:18; 14:10,19; 15:1,7; 16:1), "the time of Jacob's distress" (Jeremiah 30:7), and various other terms. Daniel 9:27 reveals that the Tribulation will be seven years in length, which is confirmed in Revelation (combine 11:3 and 12:6). The Tribulation will bring upon mankind the worst suffering and distress people have ever known. That's because it is a time during which God pours out His wrath. And the most extensive chronological account of what will happen during the Tribulation is found in the book of Revelation, in chapters 6 to 19.

The Tribulation begins after the rapture of the church with a seven-year covenant between the revived Roman Empire (comprised of a confederacy of ten European nations) and the nation of Israel (Isaiah 28:15,18; Daniel 9:24-27). Then come the seal judgments, with the first one being marked by the arrival of a rider on a white horse (Revelation 6:1-2). This represents the Antichrist's arrival on the scene. The next five seal judgments are further outpourings of wrath that take place during the earlier part of the Tribulation. Both the 144,000 Jewish male witnesses (Revelation 7:1-8; 14:1-5) and the two witnesses (Revelation 11:1-13) minister during the first half of the Tribulation, and the result is countless millions of Gentile converts and a great number of Jewish converts to the messiahship of Christ (Revelation 7:9). The Jewish temple will also be rebuilt in Jerusalem during this time, and Satan's capital will be built in Babylon. The trumpet judgments will take place in the *second* half of the first half of the Tribulation.

Many key events take place in the middle of the Tribulation. The midpoint is defined by the arrival of the abomination of desolation, whereby the Antichrist will enter the rebuilt temple and set up a statue of himself in the Holy of Holies (Daniel 9:27; Matthew 24:15; 2 Thessalonians 2:4; Revelation 13:15). The ministry of the 144,000 Jewish males appears to come to an end at the midpoint of the Tribulation.

Tribulation Timeline

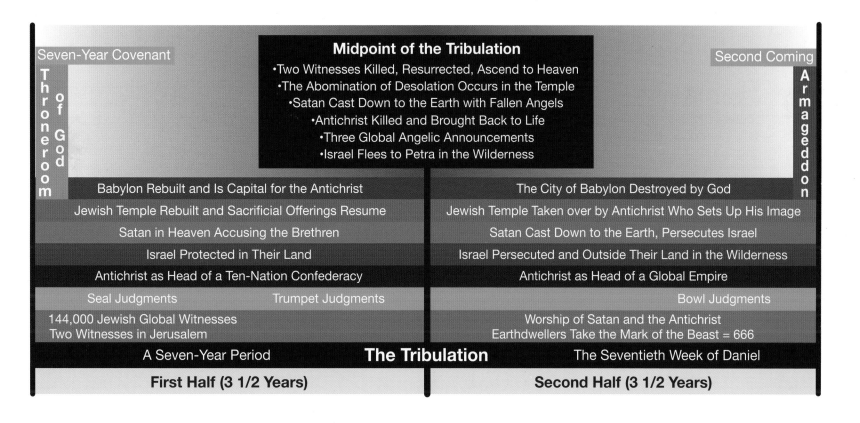

Seven-Year Covenant

Midpoint of the Tribulation
- Two Witnesses Killed, Resurrected, Ascend to Heaven
- The Abomination of Desolation Occurs in the Temple
- Satan Cast Down to the Earth with Fallen Angels
- Antichrist Killed and Brought Back to Life
- Three Global Angelic Announcements
- Israel Flees to Petra in the Wilderness

Second Coming

Throne room of God

Armageddon

First Half (3 1/2 Years)	Second Half (3 1/2 Years)
Babylon Rebuilt and Is Capital for the Antichrist	The City of Babylon Destroyed by God
Jewish Temple Rebuilt and Sacrificial Offerings Resume	Jewish Temple Taken over by Antichrist Who Sets Up His Image
Satan in Heaven Accusing the Brethren	Satan Cast Down to the Earth, Persecutes Israel
Israel Protected in Their Land	Israel Persecuted and Outside Their Land in the Wilderness
Antichrist as Head of a Ten-Nation Confederacy	Antichrist as Head of a Global Empire
Seal Judgments Trumpet Judgments	Bowl Judgments
144,000 Jewish Global Witnesses Two Witnesses in Jerusalem	Worship of Satan and the Antichrist Earthdwellers Take the Mark of the Beast = 666
A Seven-Year Period **The Tribulation** The Seventieth Week of Daniel	

And the ministry of the two witnesses comes to an abrupt end when they are killed in the middle of the Tribulation. Their bodies will lay in the street of Jerusalem, and after three-and-a-half days, they will arise and be taken up to heaven (Revelation 11:7-13). This will lead to the conversion of many Jews to the messiahship of Jesus (Revelation 11:13).

Jesus warned that when the abomination of desolation happens, the Jewish people were to flee into the wilderness because great persecution will come during the second half of the Tribulation (Matthew 24:15-21). Satan and his fallen angels will be cast out of heaven and limited to the earth (Revelation 12:7-9). Satan will then seek to persecute and wipe out the Jews, whom God will miraculously protect in the wilderness, likely at Petra (Revelation 12:13-17). The beast, as he is known in Revelation, or the Antichrist, will be killed at the midpoint and then brought back to life by God for the second half of the Tribulation (Revelation 13:3,12,14).[1] Three angelic announcements will be made to every human being upon the planet at this time (Revelation 14:6-11). The first angel will preach the gospel to every person in the world. The second angel will warn that Babylon is fallen, even though that will not happen for a few more years. The third angel will warn everyone not to take the mark of the beast (666), or they will spend eternity in the Lake of Fire.

The second half of the Tribulation will begin with the proclamation that every person on earth is required to take the mark of the beast if he wants to be able to buy or sell (Revelation 13:16-18). Those who take the mark of the beast will show that they are not among the elect (Revelation 17:8). The Antichrist will head up a global kingdom during this time and will attempt to destroy all the Jews (Revelation 12:13). At some point during the second half of the Tribulation the rebuilt city of Babylon will be destroyed by fire (Revelation 18). The seven bowl judgments will take place in rapid succession just before the end of the Tribulation, in preparation for the second coming (Revelation 16).

The Campaign of Armageddon will take place just before Christ returns to earth. Then the great and glorious appearing of our Lord will occur, bringing an end to the Tribulation (Daniel 7:13; Zechariah 14:4; Matthew 24:27-31; Revelation 19:11-16). Jesus said,

> Immediately after the tribulation of those days the sun will be darkened, and the moon will not give its light, and the stars will fall from the sky, and the powers of the heavens will be shaken, and then the sign of the Son of Man will appear in the sky, and then all the tribes of the earth will mourn, and they will see the Son of Man coming on the clouds of the sky with power and great glory (Matthew 24:29-30).

The seven-year Tribulation will end with the coming of Jesus Christ to set up His 1000-year kingdom upon earth, during which He will reign from Jerusalem.

36

THE SEQUENCE OF SECOND-COMING EVENTS

THE MOST IMPORTANT EVENT in God's prophetic plan for mankind is the physical second coming of His Son Jesus Christ. That is the event that will change this world forever. The second coming is essential to the fulfillment of Bible doctrine, for many of the great truths of Scripture would go unfulfilled without it. Just as Jesus' first coming was physical, so will be His second coming. Christ's return is clearly noted in passages such as Daniel 7:13, Zechariah 14:4, Matthew 24:27-31, and Revelation 19:11-16.

Armageddon will be the last great world war of history, and it will take place in Israel in conjunction with the second coming of Christ. The battle is described in Daniel 11:40-45, Joel 3:9-17, Zechariah 14:1-3, and Revelation 16:14-16. It will occur in the final days of the Tribulation, when the kings of the world will be gathered together "for the war of the great day of God, the Almighty" in a place known as "Har–Magedon" (Revelation 16:14,16). The site where this will occur is the plain of Esdraelon, around the hill of Megiddo, in northern Israel, about 20 miles south-southeast of Haifa.

The term *Armageddon* comes from the Hebrew tongue. *Har* is the word for "mountain" and often appears with the Hebrew definite article. *H. Mageddon* is likely the ruins of an ancient city that overlooks the Valley of Esdraelon in northern Israel.

According to the Bible, great armies from both the east and the west will gather and assemble on this plain. There will be threats to the power of the Antichrist from the south, and he will move to destroy a revived Babylon in the east before finally turning his forces toward Jerusalem to subdue and destroy it. As he and his armies approach Jerusalem, God will intervene, and Jesus Christ will return to rescue His people Israel. The Lord and His angelic army will destroy the Antichrist's armies, capture the Antichrist and the false prophet, and cast them into the Lake of Fire (Revelation 19:11-21).

In a sense, Armageddon will be a battle that never really takes place. That is, it will not take place in accordance with its original human intent—to gather the armies of the world to execute the Antichrist's "final solution" to the "Jewish problem." That is why Jesus Christ chooses this specific moment in history for His return to earth—to thwart the Antichrist's attempted annihilation of the Jews and to destroy the armies of the world, which have been gathered for another purpose. It seems only fitting, in light of mankind's bloody legacy, that the return of Christ should be precipitated by worldwide military conflict against Israel. So it is that history is moving toward Armageddon.

The Eight Stages of Armageddon[1]

1. The gathering of all the world's armies at Armageddon (Joel 3:9-11; Psalm 2:1-6; Revelation 16:12-16).

2. God destroys Babylon, Antichrist's capital (Isaiah 13–14; Jeremiah 50–51; Zechariah 5:5-11; Revelation 17–18).

3. Jerusalem is attacked and half the city falls (Micah 4:11–5:1; Zechariah 12–14).

4. The armies of the Antichrist attack the Jews hidden in Petra (Bozrah) (Jeremiah 49:13-14; Micah 2:12).

5. Israel is regenerated and accepts Jesus as their Messiah (Psalm 79:1-13; 80:1-19; Isaiah 64:1-12; Hosea 6:1-13; Joel 2:28-32; Zechariah 12:10; 13:7-9; Romans 11:25-27).

6. Jesus rescues redeemed Israel hidden away at Petra (Isaiah 34:1-7; 63:1-3; Habakkuk 3:3; Micah 2:12-13).

7. The armies of the world are destroyed at the Valley of Jehoshaphat (Jeremiah 49:20-22; Zechariah 14:12-15; Joel 3:12-13).

8. The victory ascent by Jesus upon the Mount of Olives (Zechariah 14:3-5; Joel 3:14-17; Matthew 24:29-31; Revelation 16:17-21; 19:11-21).

Sequence of Second-Coming Events

Midpoint of the Tribulation		The Second Coming of Christ
	Victory Ascent by Jesus upon the Mount of Olives in Jerusalem	
	Armies of the World Are Destroyed at the Valley of Jehoshaphat	
	Jesus Rescues Redeemed Israel Hidden Away at Petra	
	Israel Is Regenerated and Accepts Jesus as Their Messiah	
	Armies of the Antichrist Attack Jews Hidden in Petra	
	Jerusalem Attacked and Half the City Falls	
	God Destroys Babylon, Antichrist's Capital	
	Gathering of All the World's Armies at Armaggedon	
	Second Half of the Tribulation 3 1/2 Years	

37

THE MILLENNIUM

MILLENNIUM IS A LATIN TERM for "a thousand." Revelation 20:1-7 says that Christ will set up a kingdom and reign for 1000 years after His second coming (the word translated "thousand," in the New Testament, was *chilias*). Christ's millennial kingdom is the capstone of history and a precursor to eternity. During this time Jesus Christ will be the focus of all creation, and He will rule visibly over the entire world in power and great glory. It will be a wonderful time during which righteousness and peace will prevail.

It is significant to note that within the history of all human thought, it is only in the Bible, and those influenced by biblical revelation, that we find history ending in triumph. All other approaches view the slope of history as moving from their ideal as a memory of the past, trying to restore former glory in the present. This is indeed the case with everything that sinful man touches—it degenerates. Only the Bible teaches that the best is yet to come.

Many Old Testament passages speak of a yet-future time of true peace and prosperity for the righteous followers of God under the benevolent physical rule of Jesus Christ on earth. Zechariah 14:9 says, "The LORD will be king over all the earth; in that day the LORD will be the only one, and His name the only one." Then in verses 16-21 we read about what the kingdom will be like—a time when the Lord will demonstrate to humanity what the world would have been like had Adam and Eve not cast it into sin by their single act of disobedience.

There are other Old Testament passages that speak of the millennial kingdom: Psalm 2:6-9; Isaiah 2:2-4; 11:6-9; 65:18-23; Jeremiah 31:12-14,31-37; Ezekiel 34:25-29; 37:1-6; 40–48; Daniel 2:35; 7:13-14; Joel 2:21-27; Amos 9:13-14; Micah 4:1-7; and Zephaniah 3:9-20. These are only a few of the many prophetic passages that describe this kingdom even before Christ's first coming to earth.

The New Testament also speaks of the coming millennial kingdom in passages such as Matthew 5:1-20; 19:27-30; 26:27-29; Mark 14:25; Luke 22:18; 1 Corinthians 6:9-11; and Revelation 20. Interestingly, it's not until we get to Revelation that we are told the kingdom will last 1000 years, even though many passages describe what this time period will be like.

Millennial Events

75-Day Interval

- Second Coming
- Sheep and Goat Judgment

The Millennium

- Millennium Begins
- Christ Reigns in Jerusalem
- Curse Removed Except for Death
- New Temple Established
- Temple Sacrifices
- No More War
- Great Economic Prosperity
- Lifespan Will Be 1000 years
- Satan Bound
- David Is Prince over Israel
- Populated by Mortals
- Populated by Resurrected Bodies
- A Time of Peace and Prosperity
- Mortals Able to Reproduce Offspring
- Newborn Need to Accept Christ
- Egypt in Forty-Year Dispersion
- Christ Rules as Dictator
- A Time of Righteousness and Justice
- A Time of Economic Prosperity
- The Glory of Christ Will Abound
- All Jewish Mortals Will Accept Christ
- Some Gentile Children Reject Christ
- Great Agricultural Productivity
- No More Wild Animals
- A Time of Safety
- All Mortals Still Have a Sin Nature
- The Church Will Reign with Christ
- Death Against Disobedient Mortals
- God's Law Written on Human Hearts
- Nations Gather Yearly in Jerusalem
- Everything Will Be Holy to the Lord

Great White Throne Judgment

- Satan Loosed
- Satan Cast into the Lake of Fire
- Millennium Ends
- All Unbelievers Judged and Cast into the Lake of Fire
- History Ends

The major features of the Millennium are:

- the binding of Satan at the beginning of the Millennium (Revelation 20:1-3)
- the final restoration of Israel, which will include:

  —regeneration (Jeremiah 31:31-34)

  —regathering (Deuteronomy 30:1-10; Isaiah 11:11–12:6; Matthew 24:31)

  —possession of the land (Ezekiel 20:42-44; 36:28-38)

  —reestablishment of the Davidic throne (2 Samuel 7:11-16; 1 Chronicles 17:10-14; Jeremiah 33:17-26)

- the reign of Jesus Christ (Isaiah 2:3-4; 11:2-5)
- the loosing and final rebellion of Satan at the end of the Millennium (Revelation 20:7-10)
- the Great White Throne Judgment and the second resurrection or judgment of unbelieving dead (Revelation 20:11-15)

The Millennium will be a time during which the Adamic curse will be rolled back, except for death, and in which mortals will live for 1000 years. Christ will sit on the throne of David and rule the world, bringing peace and righteousness as He puts down any open rebellion with His rod of iron. The Millennium will be a time of great spiritual triumph during which national Israel will fulfill her destiny and Gentiles will partake of tremendous blessings through Jesus Christ and the nation of Israel. The Bible describes the Millennium as a time of righteousness, obedience, holiness, truth, and a fullness of the Holy Spirit as never before.

The Millennium will be a time of tremendous environmental transformation. Isaiah 35:1-2 tells us the desert will blossom and become productive. There will be abundant rainfall in areas that today are known for being arid, and there will be plenty of food for animals (Isaiah 30:23-24; 35:7). In addition, the predatory behavior of animals will cease. The distinctions between tame and wild will be erased, as all creatures will live in harmony (Isaiah 11:6-7).

For people, physical conditions will drastically change for the better. People will enjoy much longer life spans, and many physical infirmities and health concerns will be eradicated (Isaiah 29:18; 33:24). The absence of sickness and deformity—along with the increased life spans—will maximize the differences between those who still have mortal bodies and those who have resurrected bodies. In the midst of this enhanced environment, people will enjoy increased prosperity as poverty, injustice, and disease cease (Jeremiah 31:12-14).

Spiritual life in the millennial kingdom will be unlike anything we've ever experienced. Living daily in the personal and physical presence of Jesus Christ, who will sit on the Davidic throne, will have an enormous impact on the lives of believers. Isaiah said, "The earth will be full of the knowledge of the LORD as the waters cover the sea" (Isaiah 11:9). The knowledge and worship of Christ will be global and unimpeded. The Millennium will be an era of great spiritual awareness, sensitivity, and activity for Gentile believers, Christians, and the restored nation of Israel. For Israel, the New Covenant will be in effect, bringing to fruition the conditions prophesied in passages such as Isaiah 59:20-21; Jeremiah 31:31-34; 32:37-40; Ezekiel 16:60-63; and 37:21-28. Also, every Jewish person born during the Millennium will become a believer, as the Lord makes it up to them for their centuries of unbelief and disobedience (Jeremiah 31:34).

The clearest expression of the spiritual characteristics of the millennial kingdom is found in the worship and activity in the millennial temple. Jesus Christ will be reigning on earth from His throne in Jerusalem, and the millennial temple will be present and functioning as described in Ezekiel 40–46. Worship in the millennial temple will no doubt be of a quality and depth never before seen on earth, as righteous Jews and Gentiles gladly come to Jerusalem to praise the great Savior King (Isaiah 2:2-4; 11:9-10; Ezekiel 20:40-41; 40:1–46:24; Zechariah 14:16).

Unfortunately, even in the midst of such pristine conditions, there will still be human rebellion. Because the complete effects of the Fall will not have been erased, there will be one final revolt against the righteous government of Jesus Christ. This revolt will occur at the end of the Millennium, when Satan is briefly released from bondage in the abyss. He will stir up mortal, unbelieving Gentiles who will gather willingly in an uprising against the Lord. But as Scripture says, in the end, Satan will be judged and punished forever (Revelation 20:7-10).

This event will take us to the absolute end of history, after which point no more human beings will be born into this world. Those who became believers during the Millennium will receive a resurrection body that prepares them for life in eternity. And unbelievers from all throughout history will appear before the Great White Throne Judgment, be condemned, and be cast into the Lake of Fire to suffer for all eternity (verses 11-15).

In a world filled with chaos, despair, corruption, violence, and rampant evil, the certainty of the Millennium offers us assurance that God's prophetic program has not been abandoned. There really will come a day when Christ will rule the world with righteousness and justice. Evil will be judged, and believers of all ages will worship Jesus Christ in His presence. Because of this, Christians today need not have anxiety or fear. Our "blessed hope" is Jesus Christ (Titus 2:13), and we can have confidence that His kingdom will indeed come.

It is important that the millennial kingdom occur within human history and in eternity. It is important because history will conclude on a victorious note for God's plan through the second Adam, the Lord Jesus Christ. Just as Jesus was humiliated upon earth at His first coming, even though He conquered death and ascended to heaven, the final phase of His earthly presence will be one of total victory—the removal of the curse and a return to Edenic conditions for 1000 years.

Fallen humanity's rebellion against God and their ungodly culture must not be allowed to stand in history. Daniel 2:44-45 says,

> In the days of those kings the God of heaven will set up a kingdom which will never be destroyed, and that kingdom will not be left for another people; it will crush and put an end to all these kingdoms, but it will itself endure forever. Inasmuch as you saw that a stone was cut out of the mountain without hands and that it crushed the iron, the bronze, the clay, the silver, and the gold, the great God has made known to the king what will take place in the future; so the dream is true and its interpretation is trustworthy.

This passage tells us that when Christ returns and sets up the millennial kingdom, the legacy of this world will be totally destroyed and blown away as if it were mere dust.

38

GOD'S JUDGMENTS IN HISTORY AND PROPHECY

I N SPITE OF POPULAR BELIEF to the contrary, God will judge His creation because He is a righteous and just God. In fact, God has already exercised judgment many times in the past, even though some do not recognize these events (2 Peter 3:1-13). This chart shows the chronological sequence of the main judgment events in the past as well as the future.

There have been many judgments throughout history. For example, Adam and Eve were judged when they brought sin into the world by defying God and eating from the tree of the knowledge of good and evil. God's curse came upon them as well as nature, and they were kicked out of the Garden of Eden. The global flood in the days of Noah was a judgment upon sinful mankind, in which God further cursed the world and brought about changes that would affect postdiluvian humanity. God brought judgment upon Sodom and Gomorrah because both cities were filled with exceedingly wicked inhabitants who engaged in all sorts of sins, including homosexuality. The nation of Egypt experienced God's judgment via the ten plagues, after which the Israelites became free of slavery. In Genesis 15:14, we read that God

coordinated the judgment of the Canaanites with Israel's conquest of the land after the exodus. Both the Northern and Southern Kingdoms experienced judgment when each was taken into captivity by foreign nations. The Roman destruction of Jerusalem and the temple in AD 70 is said to be a judgment for the Jewish people's rejection of their Messiah (Luke 19:41-44). And there are other judgments recorded in Scripture as well.

Romans 1 teaches that God's judgment is ongoing throughout history as He gives individuals and societies over to self-destruction as they descend into idolatry (verses 21-32). For the time being, God has established civil government and nationalism as instruments for restraining evil upon the earth, for He has said He will not engage in global judgment again until His second coming (Genesis 8:20–9:7; 11:1-9; Romans 13:4-5). So God is active in our own days through His providential interaction in the daily affairs of mankind.

According to Scripture, several judgment events will take place in the future, each with a specific purpose, end, and constituency. To speak of a single all-encompassing judgment day does not line up with biblical teaching. There are different judgments for believers' sins and works, Old Testament saints, Tribulation saints, Jews living at the end of the Tribulation, Gentiles living at the end of the Tribulation, and Satan and the fallen angels. Then at the end of history comes the final judgment, which will be for all unredeemed people.

Christ's death on the cross was a past event in which God placed upon Jesus the sins of the whole world. On the cross, Christ became our substitute and paid for our sins through His death (John 5:24; Romans 8:1-4; 10:4). By bearing our sins, Christ made it possible to provide His righteous status to all who believe in Him. All who bring their sins to Christ at the cross—through simple faith—will not have to face the future judgments (except the judgment seat of Christ) because Jesus has legally paid their debt of sin in full.

Bema is the transliteration of a Greek word used in the New Testament as a technical term to distinguish the judgment of rewards for believers from the final judgment of unbelievers, which is known as the Great White Throne Judgment (Revelation 20:11-15). In the Roman world of New Testament times, there was a raised platform in the city square or at the coliseums where a dignitary would sit to hear civil matters or hand out rewards (usually a wreath) for competitive accomplishments. These platforms were known as the *bema*. Paul told the believers at the church in Corinth, "We must all appear before the judgment seat [*bema*] of Christ, so that each one may be recompensed for his deeds in the body, according to what he has done, whether good or bad" (2 Corinthians 5:10). Paul also said, "We will all stand before the judgment seat [*bema*] of God" (Romans 14:10). The judgment seat of Christ is a time of evaluation that only church-age believers will undergo.

First Corinthians 3:11-16, 4:1-5, and 9:24-27 provide extensive details about the basis on which believers will be evaluated at the *bema* judgment. Paul said in 1 Corinthians 3:11-16 that all believers have laid a foundation upon putting their trust in Christ as their Savior. Paul went on to say that each believer then builds upon that foundation with either gold, silver, and precious stones, or wood, hay, and stubble. These building materials represent the works or deeds of a believer. Because the foundation is laid by Christ Himself, it cannot be impacted by the building materials utilized by a believer. However, every believer will face a time of testing during which fire will be used to reveal the types of material he or she used as they built upon the foundation. If their deeds are constituted as gold, silver, and precious stones, then they will make it through the test of fire without being destroyed. But if their deeds are deemed to be wood, hay, and stubble, they will be burned up by fire and those believers will suffer loss of reward. This judgment will not impact a believer's salvation; rather, it will reveal whether a person has been faithful in their service to Christ. Those who have been faithful will receive rewards and crowns.

At the rapture, the church will be removed from the earth and taken up by Christ (John 14:1-3) to remain with Him in heaven all through the Tribulation (Revelation 19:1-10). The *bema* judgment will take place in heaven while the Tribulation is taking place on earth so that the church may be adorned as Christ's bride when she descends with Him at the second coming (Revelation 19:1-10). That the *bema* evaluation of the entire church takes place after the rapture but before the second coming is seen in the fact that Revelation 19:7-8 tells us that "His bride has made herself ready. It was given to her to clothe herself in fine linen, bright and clean; for the fine linen is the righteous acts of the saints." Because the church is pictured as being clothed in fine linen, we can conclude she must have gone through her evaluation, or *bema* judgment, by the time of the second coming.

Next, the Tribulation is said to be a time during which God will make Israel "pass under the rod" in order to "purge from you the rebels" (Ezekiel 20:37-38). Thus, the Tribulation is a time of judgment upon the nation of Israel, during which two-thirds of the people will die (Zechariah 13:8-9). Then, of those who are left, "all Israel will be saved" (Romans 11:26) by coming to faith in Jesus as their Messiah. The Tribulation will also be a time of judgment upon unbelieving Gentiles who have rejected Christ as their Savior (Deuteronomy 30:7; Isaiah 24–27; Revelation 3:10).

At the end of the Tribulation will come the judgment of the nations. This will be a time, according to Matthew 25:31-46, when all unbelievers will be put to death in preparation for the millennial kingdom. Only believers will populate the kingdom at its beginning, and the

God's Judgments in History and Prophecy

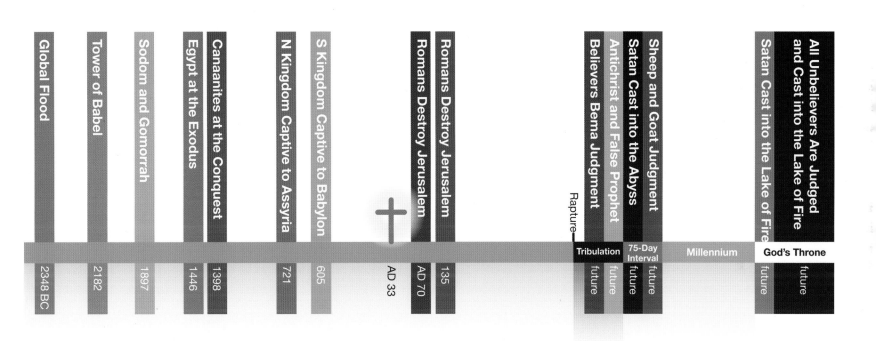

Global Flood	Tower of Babel	Sodom and Gomorrah	Egypt at the Exodus	Canaanites at the Conquest	N Kingdom Captive to Assyria	S Kingdom Captive to Babylon		Romans Destroy Jerusalem	Romans Destroy Jerusalem	Believers Bema Judgment	Antichrist and False Prophet	Satan Cast into the Abyss	Sheep and Goat Judgment		Satan Cast into the Lake of Fire	All Unbelievers Are Judged and Cast into the Lake of Fire
							Rapture									
										Tribulation	75-Day Interval		Millennium		God's Throne
2348 BC	2182	1897	1446	1398	721	605	AD 33	AD 70	135	future	future	future	future		future	future

judgment of the nations will ensure that all unbelievers are removed before the kingdom commences (Matthew 13:47-50).

The final judgment of all history is known as the Great White Throne Judgment and will involve the judgment of all unbelievers through all time (Revelation 20:11-15). It appears that all unbelievers from every dispensation—since the beginning of history—are being kept in "Sheol," as the Old Testament calls it, or "Hades," as the New Testament labels it. This would be like a person who is caught committing a crime first being taken to county or city jail and held there until his trial. Then when he is found guilty at the trial, he is transferred to the state prison to serve out his sentence.

There is not much difference between the living conditions in the local jail and the state penitentiary; however, the state prison is a different location, and it's where the criminal serves out his sentence. So it is that hell is a lot like the Lake of Fire, but they are two different locations. The Lake of Fire currently has no occupants, but it's where all unbelievers will spend all eternity for rejecting Christ as their Savior.

The Bible does not specifically state who sits on the Great White Throne, but it is probably Jesus Christ Himself (see Revelation 3:21). This judgment is the "resurrection of judgment" spoken of in John 5:29 (as opposed to the "resurrection of life"). The people who experience this judgment will be those who rejected Jesus Christ while alive on earth. Because of their rejection of Christ's substitutionary work, God will judge them on the basis of their own works, which will fail to measure up to His standard of perfect holiness. In this judgment, their works will reveal that the punishment is deserved, and afterward, these people will be thrown into the Lake of Fire for eternity.

Though we often hear people speak of a single judgment day, this is not biblically accurate, for there are several future judgments in God's prophetic plan. These judgments will occur at various times between the rapture and the end of the Millennium, and they are certain and no one will escape them. They will make manifest God's justice and righteousness to the entire world and will silence all who have scoffed at or denied God.

39

THE RESURRECTIONS IN HISTORY AND PROPHECY

THERE IS COMING A TIME when God will renew the creation and resurrect all mankind, some to everlasting life and the rest to eternal death (John 5:29). In fact, the transition from the current creation to the new heavens and new earth (as stated in Revelation 21–22) is viewed as a resurrection of creation, which, at the time of Adam and Eve's fall, had come under the curse of sin (Matthew 19:28; Revelation 21:1). The apostle Paul spoke of a chronology involving the resurrection when he said, "But each in his own order: Christ the first fruits, after that those who are Christ's at His coming" (1 Corinthians 15:23). We have included in this chapter a chart that records the different times in history when resurrection events have occurred.

The concept of future bodily resurrection is found throughout the Bible. It is important to note that, in Scripture, the word *resurrection* is used solely to refer to the raising up of the physical body. There is no such thing as a spiritual resurrection. When the Bible speaks of the spiritual newness of a person who has become a believer in Christ Jesus, it uses the imagery of a new birth (John 3:3; Ephesians 2:5), not that of a resurrection. When the New Testament speaks of a believer having been "raised up" with Christ (Ephesians 2:6; Colossians 3:1-2), it speaks of one's position in Christ at the right hand of the Father, not a resurrection.

The resurrections in Scripture fall into two categories: the first resurrection or the resurrection of life; and the second resurrection or the resurrection of judgment (John 5:28-29).

The first resurrection includes the redeemed of all ages. The timing of the resurrection of these individuals varies, depending upon whether they are an Old Testament saint (Jew or Gentile), a Christian living before or at the time of the rapture, or a Christian who is martyred during the Tribulation period. All these people will take part in the "resurrection of life" (John 5:29), even though those resurrections will occur at different times throughout history, as noted in the chart.

The second resurrection, or "resurrection of judgment," will include the unredeemed of all the ages. They will be raised at the end of the Millennium in a single event, judged before the Great White Throne, and cast into the Lake of Fire.

The multiple resurrections will take place in this sequence:

1. The resurrection of Jesus Christ as the first fruit of many to be raised (Romans 6:9; 1 Corinthians 15:23; Colossians 1:18; Revelation 1:18).

2. The resurrection of the redeemed at Christ's coming (Daniel 12:2; Luke 14:14; John 5:29; 1 Thessalonians 4:16; Revelation 20:4,6).

   a. The resurrection of the church at the rapture.

   b. The resurrection of Old Testament believers at the second coming (saved Jews and Gentiles).

   c. The resurrection of all martyred Tribulation saints at the second coming (saved Jews and Gentiles).

   d. The resurrection of all millennial believers after the Millennium.

3. The resurrection of the unredeemed (Revelation 20:11-14).

Resurrections in History and Prophecy

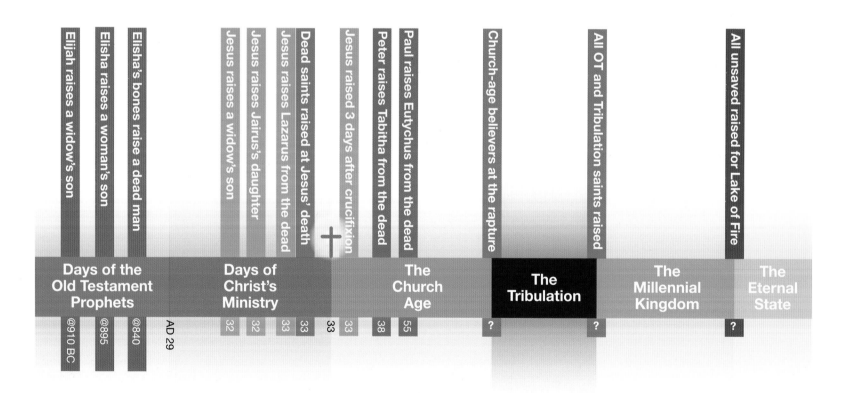

Elijah raises a widow's son
Elisha raises a woman's son
Elisha's bones raise a dead man
Jesus raises a widow's son
Jesus raises Jairus's daughter
Jesus raises Lazarus from the dead
Dead saints raised at Jesus' death
Jesus raised 3 days after crucifixion
Peter raises Tabitha from the dead
Paul raises Eutychus from the dead
Church-age believers at the rapture
All OT and Tribulation saints raised
All unsaved raised for Lake of Fire

Days of the Old Testament Prophets — @910 BC, @895, @840

Days of Christ's Ministry — AD 29, 32, 32, 33

The Church Age — 33, 33, 38, 55

The Tribulation — ?

The Millennial Kingdom — ?

The Eternal State — ?

40

WHAT IS YOUR CHOICE?

IT SHOULD BE CLEAR BY NOW that God loves mankind and has a wonderful plan for the future of those whose trust Jesus as their Savior. It is called heaven, and it is eternal. We have seen in this book that God has a plan for history as recorded in Scripture. His plan has a beginning and also an end. Each one of us as individuals also have a beginning and an ending of this life. However, the Bible clearly teaches that there is an eternity for all humanity beyond history. Thus, you will spend eternity in one of two places: either in heaven or hell. Eternity is a long, long, long time! This fact should be a sobering thought for any individual to contemplate. And it is why God is giving everyone an opportunity to choose whether they will spend eternity with Him and other believers in heaven or separated from Him for all eternity in the Lake of Fire.

That God truly loves us is clearly evident because He sent "His only begotten Son" into the world to die on the cross for our sins. Had He not done so, no one would ever know redemption from their sins and enjoy the blessings of an abundant and meaningful life in history and forever in heaven.

Some people wonder why their eternal destination is an either/or choice. It's because God is a multifaceted being—He is both loving as well as righteous and just. All aspects of His being work together in perfect harmony, and He cannot contradict or compromise any of His attributes. Because He is righteous, His standards are always the right standards. Because He is just, He cannot do anything that is unjust. Therefore, He must punish sin—He cannot "look the other way" and let us enter heaven with our sins unaccounted for. His love found a way to provide salvation for humanity: Through the death of His perfect Son on the cross. Because Christ paid the penalty, you can place your trust in what Christ did for you, and be declared righteous by God. That is why Paul was able to say of God in Romans 3:23 that He is "just and the justifier of the one who has faith in Jesus." Love and justice were perfectly balanced through God's provision of salvation to sinful people.

Because Adam and Eve chose to disobey God, sin entered into the human race and was passed on to all mankind. Sin created a chasm between God and man that could not be bridged until His divine and

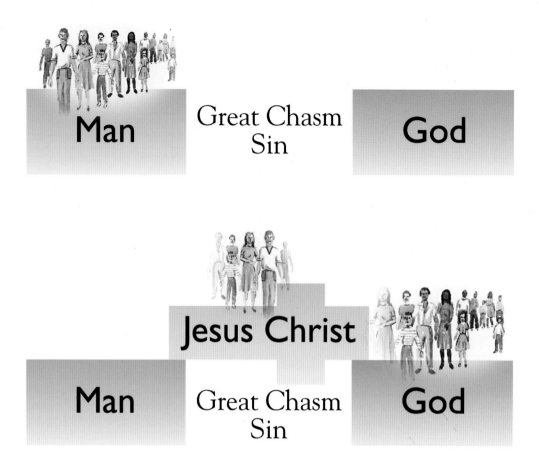

holy Son, Jesus, identified with the human race by becoming one of us through the virgin birth. This made it possible for a holy God to not only identify with us, but become the sacrifice for our sins through His substitutionary death on the cross. His bodily resurrection was God's way of proving to all mankind that He accepted His Son's sacrifice for all humanity.

Because of what happened at the cross, it is possible for people to come back to God by trusting Christ personally to forgive their sins and restore the broken relationship between themselves and God. Just like the decision a person makes to walk out on a bridge to cross a chasm, the choice to trust Christ is an individual matter. No one else can do it for you. When it comes to trusting Christ, every person must make his or her own decision.

Those who choose to trust Christ and His sacrificial provision will enter heaven. Those who do not choose Him will die in their sins, be judged, and then sent to the eternal Lake of Fire.

It is no exaggeration, then, to say that the choice you make about trusting Jesus Christ is the most important decision you will ever make on this earth. Have you personally trusted Jesus to forgive your sins and provide you with eternal life? The moment your mind turns from rejection of Christ to belief or trust in Him and His provision, you become a believer and are transferred from darkness into the light.

Don't miss this so great offer of eternal salvation—believe on the Lord Jesus Christ today, and you will be saved!

NOTES

Chapter 1—Why a Chart Book on Bible Chronology?

1. W.F. Arndt, F.W. Danker, F.W. Gingrich, & Walter Bauer, *A Greek-English Lexicon of the New Testament and Other Early Christian Literature*, 3rd ed. (Chicago: University of Chicago Press, 2000), p. 372.

Chapter 2—How We Got Our Bible

1. Josh McDowell, *God-Breathed: The Undeniable Power and Reliability of Scripture* (Uhrichsville, OH: Shiloh Run Press, 2015), p. 154.

Chapter 5—The Divine Institutions

1. Charles A. Clough, *Laying the Foundation*, rev. ed. (Lubbock, TX: Lubbock Bible Church, 1977), p. 36.

2. Clough, *Laying*, p. 36, f.n. 36.

3. Charles A. Clough, *A Biblical Framework for Worship and Obedience in an Age of Global Deception*, Part II, p. 39. From the following internet address: http://www.cclough.com/notes.php.

4. Clough, *Biblical Framework*, p. 60.

5. Clough, *Biblical Framework*, p. 40.

6. Clough, *Laying*, p. 37.

7. Clough, *Biblical Framework*, p. 40.

8. Clough, *Biblical Framework*, p. 41.

9. Clough, *Laying*, p. 37.

10. Clough, *Biblical Framework*, p. 41.

11. Clough, *Biblical Framework*, p. 61.

12. See Clough, *Laying*, p. 83 and *Biblical Framework*, pp. 97-98.

Chapter 7—The Covenants

1. Arnold G. Fruchtenbaum, *Israelology: The Missing Link in Systematic Theology* (Tustin, CA: Ariel Ministries Press, 1993), p. 570.

Chapter 9—The Dispensations

1. Charles C. Ryrie, *Dispensationalism* (Chicago: Moody Press, 1995), pp. 25-26.

2. Ryrie, *Dispensationalism*, p. 25.

3. Ryrie, *Dispensationalism*, pp. 25-26.

4. Ryrie, *Dispensationalism*, pp. 26-27.

5. Ryrie, *Dispensationalism*, p. 28.

6. Ryrie, *Dispensationalism*, pp. 29-31.

7. Ryrie, *Dispensationalism*, p. 41.

Chapter 11-Exponential Decay Curve

1. Charles A. Clough, *Laying the Foundation*, 2nd ed. (Lubbock, TX: Lubbock Bible Church, 1977), p. 75.

2. Clough, *Laying the Foundation*, pp. 75-76.

3. Charles A. Clough, *A Biblical Framework for Worship and Obedience in an Age of Global Deception*. Part II: Buried Truths of Origins (unpublished notes, www.bibleframework.com), p. 84.

Chapter 15—From Bondage to the Exodus

1. Rameses II (1290–1223 BC) was one of Egypt's greatest Pharaohs. He ruled for 67 years and was known for his personal heroics leading his armies into battle. He was succeeded by his thirteenth son, Merneptah (1223–1214 BC), who records dealing with "Israel" in the land of Canaan. Despite attempts by those who date the exodus during the reign of Rameses, it is utterly unlikely that he was the Pharaoh of the exodus. See C.F. Aling, *Egypt and Bible History* (Grand Rapids: Baker, 1981).

Chapter 18—The Feasts of Israel in Bible Prophecy

1. Terry C. Hulbert, "The Eschatological Significance of Israel's Annual Feasts," ThD dissertation from Dallas Theological Seminary, 1965, p. 2.
2. Hulbert, "Eschatological Significance," pp. 2-3.
3. Hulbert, "Eschatological Significance," pp. 115-16.

Chapter 19—Israel's Prophetic Outline in Deuteronomy 4

1. George M. Harton, "Fulfillment of Deuteronomy 28-30 in History and Eschatology" (ThD dissertation, Dallas Theological Seminary, 1981), p. 24.

Chapter 20—Conquest and Chaos

1. For a detailed discussion of the dating of Joshua, see Marten Woudstra, *The Book of Joshua*, NICOT (Grand Rapids: Eerdmans, 1981), pp. 5-25; Bryant Wood, "The Biblical Data for the Exodus is 1446 BC," *JETS*, 50, no.2 (June 2007): 249-58.
2. See Ed Hindson and Gary Yates, *The Essence of the Old Testament: A Survey* (Nashville, TN: B&H, 2012), 138-49.

Chapter 23—Old Testament Prophets

1. Outlines of the major and minor prophets are from Ed Hindson and Gary Yates, *The Essence of the Old Testament: A Survey* (Nashville, TN: B&H, 2012), pp. 291, 367.
2. Some conservative scholars date Obadiah later, closer to the time of Jeremiah, Ibid., 393. Cf. John MacArthur, *MacArthur Bible Handbook* (Nashville, TN: Thomas Nelson, 2003), p. 279.

Chapter 26—Daniel's Prophetic Timeline

1. John F. Walvoord, *The Prophecy Knowledge Handbook* (Wheaton, IL: Scripture Press Publishing, Inc., 1990), p. 233.

Chapter 27—The 70 Weeks of Daniel

1. Harold Hoehner, *Chronological Aspects of the Life of Christ* (Grand Rapids: Zondervan, 1977), p. 139.
2. Leon Wood, *A Commentary on Daniel* (Grand Rapids: Zondervan, 1973), p. 255.
3. Robert Culver, *Daniel and the Latter Days* (Chicago: Moody Press, 1977), p. 157.
4. Steven R. Miller, *Daniel*, Vol. 18 of The New American Commentary (Nashville: Broadman & Holman, 1994), p. 267.
5. G.H. Lang, *The Histories and Prophecies of Daniel* (Miami Springs, FL: Conley & Schoettle Publishing Co., 1985), p. 135.
6. Randall Price, *Prophecy of Daniel 9:27* (San Marcos, TX: World of the Bible, n.d.), p. 22.

Chapter 32—New Testament Letters

1. Merrill C. Tenney, *New Testament Survey* (Grand Rapids: Eerdmans, 1961), p. 339.
2. E.J. Goodspeed, *An Introduction to the New Testament* (Chicago: University of Chicago Press, n.d.), pp. 319-320.
3. Tenney, *New Testament Survey*, p. 381.

Chapter 33—Book of Revelation Timeline

1. Arnold G. Fruchtenbaum, *The Footsteps of the Messiah: A Study of the Sequence of Prophetic Events*, rev. ed. (San Antonio, TX: Ariel Press, 2003), pp. 801–08.

Chapter 35—The Tribulation Timeline

1. The Antichrist's death and resurrection is clearly stated in Revelation 13:12, which, when speaking of the false prophet, says, "He makes the earth and those who dwell in it to worship the first beast whose fatal wound was healed." This language is repeated in 13:3,14; 17:8,11 for a total of five times in the book of Revelation. How is this possible, since Satan cannot raise anyone from the dead? Apparently God will raise him from the dead as part of a temporary authority given to Satan for the purpose of performing false signs and wonders in order to deceive unbelievers during the Tribulation (2 Thessalonians 2:8-12; Revelation 13:13-15). The language used to describe the death and resurrection of the Antichrist in Revelation 13:3,12,14 is the same description in the original Greek of Christ's death and resurrection (Revelation 2:8). For a more detailed presentation and defense of this view, see Mark Hitchcock and Thomas Ice, *Breaking the Apocalypse Code: Setting the Record Straight About the End Times* (Costa Mesa, CA: The Word for Today, 2007), pp. 101-13.

Chapter 36—The Sequence of Second-Coming Events

1. The Eight Stages of Armageddon are adopted from Arnold G. Fruchtenbaum, *Footsteps of the Messiah: A Study of the Sequence of Prophetic Events*, rev. ed. (San Antonio, TX: Ariel Press, 2003), pp. 314-63.

To learn more about Harvest House books and
to read sample chapters, visit our website:

www.harvesthousepublishers.com

HARVEST HOUSE PUBLISHERS
EUGENE, OREGON